To David,
Happy Birthday!

Love from Sister

XXX

2006

Help Yourself with the Kumars

Helped into print by Suk Pannu

First published in hardback in Great Britain in 2006 by Orion Books,
an imprint of the Orion Publishing Group Ltd
Orion House,
5 Upper St Martin's Lane,
London WC2H 9EA

10 9 8 7 6 5 4 3 2 1

A CIP catalogue record for this book is available from the British Library.

ISBN-13: 978 0 75287 643 6
ISBN-10: 0 75287 643 0

Designed and typeset by Smith & Gilmour, London
Printed in Italy by Rotolito Lombarda SpA'

The Orion Publishing Group's policy is to use papers that are natural,
renewable and recyclable and made from wood grown in sustainable
forests. The logging and manufacturing processes are expected to
conform to the environmental regulations of the country of origin.

www.orionbooks.co.uk

Contents

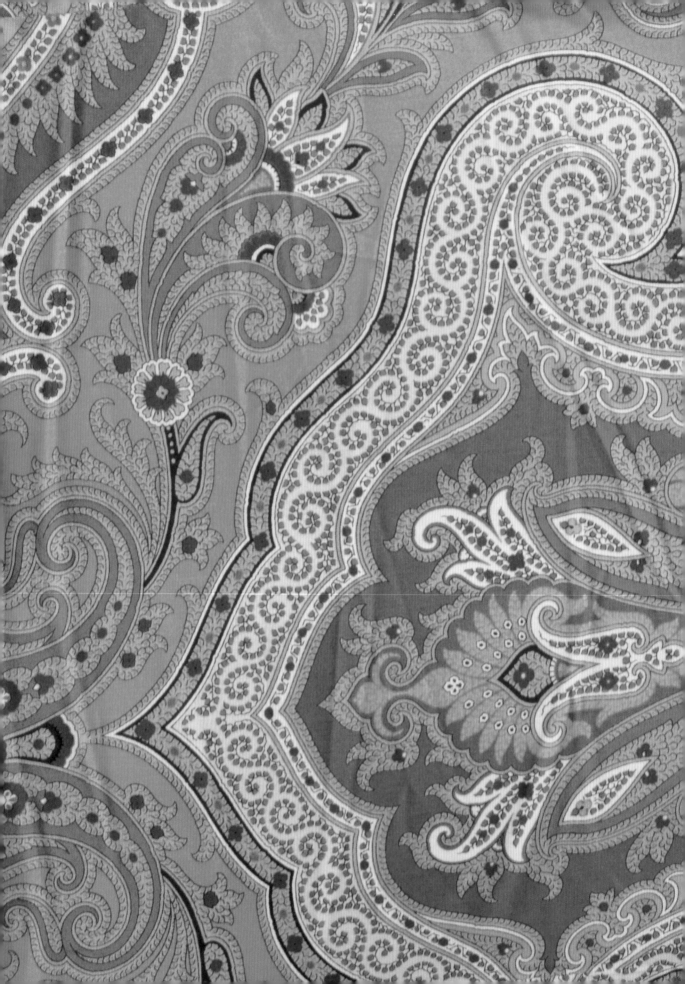

Foreword

Sanjeev Kumar

Hi ya! Sanjeev here to tell you all about this book. *Help Yourself* is the ultimate book for people who want help in their lives. I'm not saying it's for nutters, but maybe you've had a tough time with relationships, or you were an only child. Not that there's anything weird about being an only child, I am one myself, and we all go through a dry patch with the ladies sooner or later – it doesn't mean I'm gay. Look, let's stop discussing my personal life and get back to this book. It's for people who want the unique Kumars' philosophy on making friends, keeping friends and doing whatever you do with friends once you've got them. And the great thing is, each section is written by a different member of my family. It's a bit like having different sauces for a hot dog. Ketchup, mustard, brown sauce and mayonnaise. You can choose which one you prefer or, if you're like me, you mix them all up and lay it on thick. I call it Sanjy Sauce – I could eat anything with a bit of that on top. Anyway, if you're a happening thirtysomething who can't keep the chicks away, read my sections about things like 'being cool' or 'being allowed to stay up late'. I'm off now for a quick hot dog.

Ashwin Kumar

Hello, it's Ashwin. Better known to you as 'Dad', the crazy one from TV's *Kumars at No 42*. You're probably wondering what I am doing in a book like this. I bet you expected me to have my own madcap spin-off show by now – something about book-keeping or boiler maintenance. Well, you were wrong and I'm as bitterly disappointed as you are about it. The BBC simply would not buy into a drama about a central heating engineer who goes back in time after an accident in a desperate attempt to VAT register himself before submitting his tax return. It was even set in the seventies, before boilers were hidebound by all these modern rules and regulations. If you wanted to change a valve on a Twin-flow 800, you went and did it – CORGI registration be damned! The show even had a thumping soundtrack composed of all the 'Stars on 45' records. But it was not to be. So instead, I've staunched the bloody wound of my severed ambitions by offering you, the reader, advice on how to meet friends and get DIY tasks done in record time.

Madhuri Kumar

I am Madhuri Kumar, homemaker. And that's what
I will be sharing with you in this book: my own take
on making your home as lovely as possible for people
who might come round. I've got tips on cleaning up,
recipe ideas, tips for cleaning up after the recipes and
recipes on how to clean up. I want to prove once and
for all that the world of the homemaker isn't just a
one-dimensional round of cooking and cleaning.
There's a bit of laundry too! Join me as I explore
these fascinating topics.

Ummi

Hi-de-ho campers! With the population of this country becoming older and older, it's high time that the opinions of us 'oldies' were sought out. And that's exactly the way it was with this book. When the rest of the family started writing it, the first thing they did was come to me. They told me to stay out the way and go to my room. But I insisted on being involved and when they turned me away again, I used that master stroke of elderly diplomacy – crying like a baby. I wailed, beating my breast and tearing out my hair. Eventually they agreed to let me write a bit and I cut the waterworks. So wherever you see the sign of Ummi, there's oak matured guidance on friendship, romance and knitting.

Chapter one
Where to meet people

Cultural differences – Namaste

Sanjeev Kumar

The problem of meeting people is different for each and every one of us. In my case, I find that one of the best places to meet people is in my own house. This is because I have my own TV show and an enormous number of celebrities pass through my doors.

You probably don't have your own TV show – unless you're Parky or Rossy. If you are Parky or Rossy, read the next bit: Alright, mate? Drop me a line some time and we'll do coffee. If you're not Parky or Rossy, read from here. You don't have your own TV show, so the sort of people you'll be getting in will be relatives, friends, gas meter readers. That level of person. But whoever they are, don't feel you're too important to say hello to them. Whoever I get through the door, be it an Alan Alda or just a common or garden Richard E Grant, I take the time to greet them.

So let's get to greetings. You could just say 'Greetings!' but, unless you're dealing with someone Shakespearean like Captain Picard, don't do this because you look a bit weird and Victorian. So the thing is to be sensitive to other people's cultural ways of saying hello. If you meet an Irish person they might try winking and saying 'Begorrah', which is Irish for 'Hi'. Or an American would say 'Howdy Doody', or they might do the Fonzie thumbs up and say 'Heeeeey'. There are probably alien planets where they do everything psychically with their brains, so someone would say 'Hello', and it would sound like it was inside your own head. Magic!

But one of the problems the Kumars have in greeting people is that we are from an Asian extraction, and not all the stars we get coming to our house are also from an Asian extraction. This means they are not all familiar with the traditional Indian welcome known as the 'Namaste'.

The Namaste involves putting your hands together and bowing. Now when you bow, make sure you keep your eyes on the guest. Do you remember that James Bond film where there's a karate tournament and one bloke does the karate bow and the other bloke kicks him in the head because he's not looking? It's a lesson to us all. It's very unlikely one of your guests is going to kick you in the head, but they might steal something or pick their nose, so stay sharp!

Don't get kicked in the head.

The other part of the Namaste is putting the hands together. Now the firmness of your Namaste is very important. Too limp and people think you're a pussy, too firm and it looks like you're compensating for being gay. Which I'm not, whatever Ummi says. As a rough guide, pretend you're holding a BLT sandwich between your palms firmly enough to stop the lettuce falling out – but not so hard that you squeeze any of the ketchup out.

Finish off the whole thing by saying 'Namaste'. It's easy to forget this while bowing, keeping your eyes on them and trying not to think about a real BLT sandwich but it's vital. If you've done all the above and not said 'Namaste' you haven't really done a 'Namaste'. You've just bowed and put your hands together. In fact you may as well be eating a BLT sandwich … with extra mayonnaise and a nice cup of tea, thank you very much. Sorry, I drifted off there. Point is, say 'Namaste'.

This may seem quite complicated, and you may be thinking 'I'm not Indian, why would I want to do this?' or even 'what about that sandwich you keep talking about?'. But the Namaste offers a number of modern variations that shaking hands or high fiving don't.

Paper, scissor, stone, Namaste
Adds a competitive edge to the famous Indian greeting.

Quick Namaste

There's no real bow with this one, so it's light and informal. Good after a heavy meal.

Standard Namaste

This is the classic, very impressive. Good for business meetings, relatives who might have money and of course other celebrities (if you're not a celebrity – this doesn't apply to you. If you are – wotcha!).

Namaste with pull away

One for the practical joker. I find this makes me hilarious at parties.

Namaste with slapsies

Be quick on the draw – it hurts. It really does.

These are just a few of the variations, but with a little work and practice I'm sure you can develop some of your own. Happy Namaste-ing!

Knitting classes

Ummi

My attitude to meeting people is simple. What's my best chance of striking up a conversation with someone? And the answer is criticising them. Ladies, you will never have a better chance to run down a fellow pensioner than having a go at their knitting.

I first started going to knitting classes as a way of relaxing and getting away from Sanjeev's malodorous company for an evening. But my pastime has given me stimulating company and even blossomed into some real friendships. There is something about knitting that brings out the best type of female camaraderie. Yes, it's all girls together down at knitting club (if you don't count Mr Das from the hairdresser's), and we do what old ladies do best. Put the boot in. I always start slowly, by taking a friendly interest in what the person next to me is doing. Then I point out a few dropped stitches and after a while criticise their choice of wool, the colour and pointlessness of the garment. Then the killer blow: how much the treasured grandchild who gets it will inevitably hate it. At this point the gloves are off and you can follow up with personal comments about their appearance if you like. Either way, the ensuing hoo-haa will give the whole class something to talk about for the next month.

The club does its best to reach out to people from all walks of life, not just old ladies and effeminate men. As a result, very occasionally someone under the age of fifty will join. It always causes quite a stir when this happens as they can tell you about new music, what's going on in the outside world, exciting developments in their personal lives. The best thing to do is grab this opportunity with both hands and tell them to shut up. You've lived for much longer than them, why should you have to listen to them twittering on about how great The Kaiser Chiefs are and what sort of trousers to wear to a rave. Make them listen to you talking about your arthritis or how you have to wee seven times a night. If you do enough of this they soon leave, proving your point that the younger generation are weak-willed and have no real gumption, giving the whole class something to talk about for the next month.

Another thing we did at knitting club that really brought people together was 'the patchwork quilt of grandmotherhood'. Everyone had to knit a patch to represent each of their grandchildren. My patch for Sanjeev was much larger than everyone else's and of course covered in ketchup stains. Plus, I used a double knit to give it that extra weight which evokes Sanjeev in my mind. It was all going so well and then Sharda Patel had to ruin the whole quilt by crocheting anti-globalist obscenities in Urdu onto her bit. She's become a bit of an activist in recent years, and she keeps arranging 'sit-ins'. Well she would, with her hip. Anyway, she knitted an oil company logo and burnt it on the premises so we had armed police surrounding the place for four hours until she gave herself up. Still, it gave the group something to talk about for the rest of the month.

At the car showroom
Ashwin Kumar

Where is the best place to meet like-minded people who are open to new friends? I know what you're thinking. DIY store. Wrong. Men in DIY stores are far too intent on the business of buying power tools to make eye contact. Men only truly relax on two occasions. The first is after pleasing their wives ... but how often are you going to mow the lawn? Once a fortnight in summer, never in winter. The other is in car showrooms. I've often wondered why this should be. Is it right that I feel the need to make Madhuri happy before feeling relaxed? That's why the car showroom is simpler – no questions, no guilt.

Now you need to remember that there is one group of people in a car showroom you can eliminate immediately, because they will never ever be your friends: the mechanics. I have tried repeatedly standing with my mechanic while he fixes my car, offering helpful advice on what he's doing wrong. I know my Haynes manual inside out so I'm no stranger to the torque settings required for my head gasket. But these people seem to take this as an affront. What arrogance. I mean if they walked into my warehouse and gave me advice on stock handling procedures, do you think I'd snort in their faces and then drop a spanner on their feet?

Now, the choice of car showroom is dependent on the type of friend you want to make. Mercedes, Jaguar and BMW for the top end of the market – someone impressive and smooth – someone you can introduce at the Rotary Club or Business Association. Honda and Hyundai for a nice run-about who won't cost you the earth. The sort of friend who fits easily into an awkward space like a dinner party but can be discarded when you are done with them. But my favourite friends are to be found in Ford and Toyota showrooms. Functional and joyously practical, they like to keep costs down. The sort of man who appreciates a good dealer network and cheap parts is someone you want as a friend. And he could be someone that in the future you might want to share more than just words with. The type of man you'd want to do an oil change with.

So you've chosen your showroom. You've had some of the free coffee and a biscuit and you can see your potential new friend eyeing up a motor vehicle. What's the best way to open up conversation? Here are my top opening topics to get friendly in a car showroom:

'I had one of these once...'

A description of the misery or joy you experienced in owning the same model is a fascinating and informative way to get the ball rolling. Detail is the key, and memories of tricky gear transitions, clutch wear and uneven braking will definitely win you kudos.

Boot space

This is one of those make or break issues. To start a conversation with this is risky because it inflames so many passions in so many people. But on the other hand, if you can't agree on the ideal size of a car boot, are you ever going to be any more than acquaintances?

CD changers

I think they're pointless. I can change a CD, so why do I need a machine to do it? Don't get me started on this sort of thing, I go ape.

Trim

Again, this is a hot topic and pushes all the buttons. For me, unless leather comes as standard I'll stick with velour, thank you very much. I'm not paying extra just for a bit of cowhide and a square inch of wood veneer on the ash tray cover. I don't want to hear any nonsense about the feel of leather being worth the cost. I'd wear velour shoes if I could find them.

But you have to accept that other people may feel differently on these subjects, so if these topics come up in conversation, just 'agree to disagree'. Also, remember you can make enemies in a car showroom as well as friends. Big enemies. I remember a particularly bad altercation with a gentleman in a VW dealership. It was, predictably, about the pros and cons of alloy wheels. He actually thought they made the car go faster. I argued that they were a superficial feature and a needless expense. Well, I should have just left it there, but things turned personal. I questioned his knowledge of automobile mechanics and he lost it. He ended up chasing me round the estate car section waving a rolled up paint colour chart. It was very embarrassing.

Meeting people on the Internet

Sushila Kumar

The Internet is a boon for the infirm and elderly like me. What other medium gives access to cheap thermal underwear, fantastic news and pictures of hot boys in their pants? I don't mind telling you that since I discovered the Internet, I haven't had to reach for my well-worn Littlewoods catalogue once. It's gathering dust under the bed.

The Internet has made many other forms of entertainment redundant.

But let us get to the nitty gritty. We don't go on the Internet just to hunt down a cardigan bargain on eBay, though there are some excellent deals to be had; we go out there to make new friends. I like to break these new friends into two categories: people who I have no intention of meeting and men.

Let us deal with the ones I'm never going to meet first. There are any number of people out there desperately groping for friendship in a world that doesn't seem to have time for them. Many of them are old, grossly obese or just plain mad, but that shouldn't stop you from keeping in contact with them through chat rooms and generally winding them up. In fact, you can have many friendships with the same person but under different guises. One housebound, twenty-two-stone lady in Texas thinks I am Chloe, a twenty-two-year-old girl who's really into the Arctic Monkeys. But also Roger, an independent film producer with a loft apartment in Clerkenwell. Crazy!

Coincidentally, both Roger and Chloe are flying to Texas next June for a visit, but I'm planning for Chloe to run Roger over in a freak accident on the way to the airport and then be too upset to get on the plane.

This highlights the importance of honesty in your Internet dealings, because when it comes to Internet dating you won't get away with just lying. You have to be clever about it.

Wembley Connections

Name: Sushila

Profile: I love making love at midnight and getting caught in the rain … hold on, I've heard that somewhere before. I'm not used to the keyboard. How do I delete things? %^,,,,+=&&&. I'll just have to carry on.

What I really like is watching films, and asking what's going on, food that's easy to chew, men who speak up for themselves. In fact, men who just speak up. And of course good conversation – but let's face it, who has any these days? I hate just about everything: bright lights, electric cookers, plastic packaging, mobile phones, modern music, the new kinds of surgical supports and particularly overweight grandchildren.

Age: 32

This netted me a few very interesting replies as you can see below.

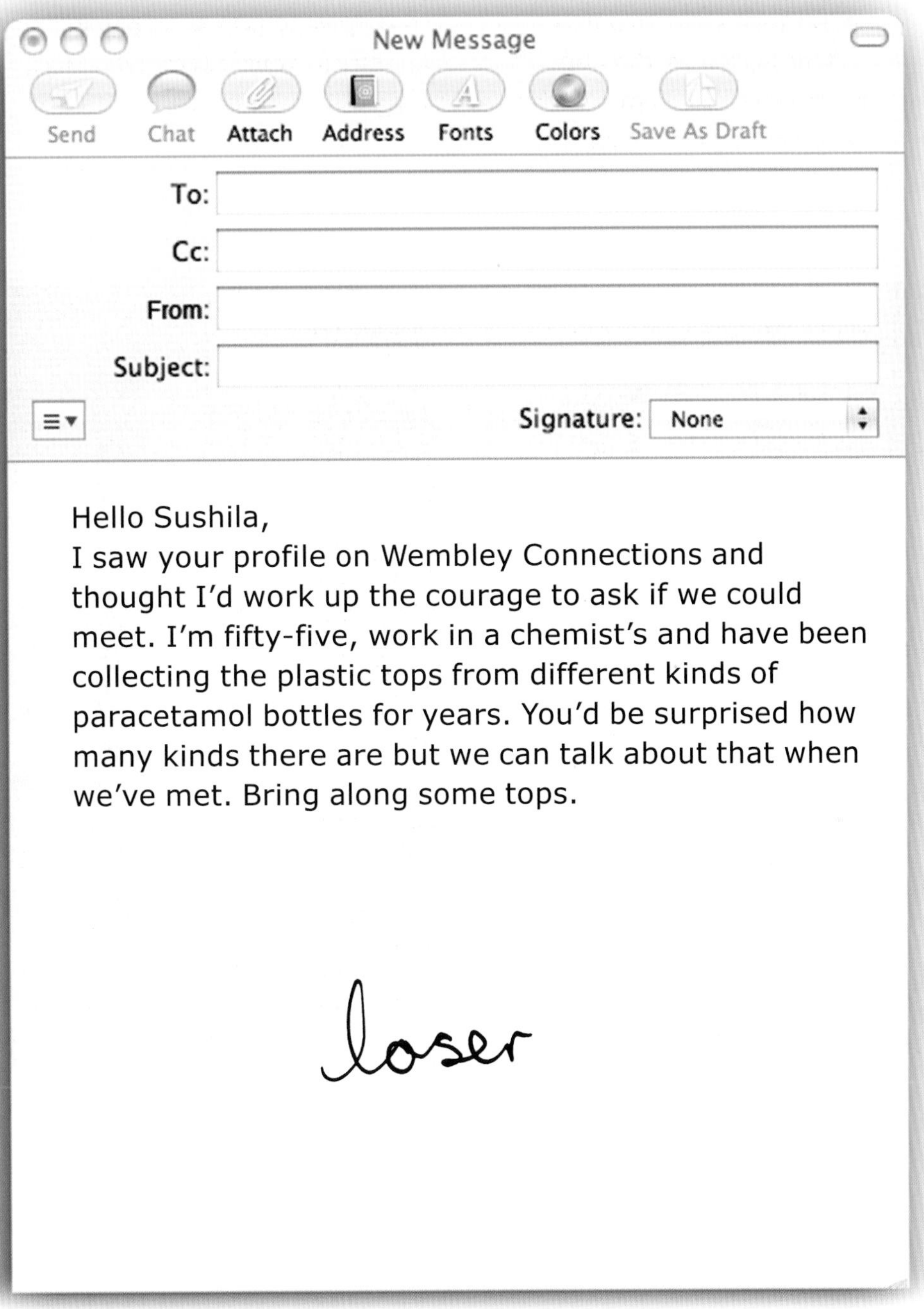

New Message

Send | Chat | Attach | Address | Fonts | Colors | Save As Draft

To:

Cc:

From:

Subject:

Signature: None

Hello Sushila,
I saw your profile on Wembley Connections and thought I'd work up the courage to ask if we could meet. I'm fifty-five, work in a chemist's and have been collecting the plastic tops from different kinds of paracetamol bottles for years. You'd be surprised how many kinds there are but we can talk about that when we've met. Bring along some tops.

loser

Send Chat Attach Address Fonts Colors Save As Draft

To:

Cc:

From:

Subject:

Signature: None

Hi Sushila,
I read your profile and am very interested in meeting you. Perhaps we could go to the cinema or even a stage play. I am a great fan of musicals and own all the recordings of Doris Day. I also like jumping in puddles, sleeping naked and watching *Will and Grace*. How about you?

might pass this onto Sanjeev

New Message

Send · Chat · Attach · Address · Fonts · Colors · Save As Draft

To:

Cc:

From:

Subject:

Signature: None

Dearest Sushila,
I really liked the look of your details on Wembley
Connections. You really are a most attractive woman.
I'm a local man and I own a successful business.
I like cars, DIY, accountancy, anything fun. I'm looking
for some friendship, someone to share my joys and
troubles with, no sordid stuff, just conversation. I am
married so I'd be very grateful for discretion. By an
incredible coincidence you share the same name as
my mother, though you look nothing like her.
Yours truly,
AK

Oh my God !!!! .

It turned out not to be Ashwin, thank goodness. But for a while there
I was truly disgusted. And I was hoping to blackmail a Stannah out of
him on the back of it. Still, the main thing is that by using the Internet
you can meet a number of people of varying degrees of interest and
availability. The following reply is the one I treasure most.

Send   Chat   Attach   Address   Fonts   Colors   Save As Draft

To:	
Cc:	
From:	
Subject:	

Signature: None

Hi Sushila,
Or can I call you Sushi? I'm thirty-two years old, own
a successful law practice and have abdominal muscles
you could play like a xylophone. I can't wait to meet
you, but the only problem is that I live in Manchester,
in my penthouse apartment, so we'd have to meet at
a motorway service station. Up for it?
Trevor

Bingo!

When I got there Trevor was a sixty-three-year-old man with halitosis and random facial hair. And he had the nerve to accuse *me* of doctoring my photo! Anyway, after a long journey I thought I should at least stay for a cup of tea and a chat and he was actually very charming in an old-fashioned way. He worked at the motorway service station as a cleaner but that didn't worry me. We were both past our prime but fed up of people thinking there was no adventure left in us. After a bit he told me he had the keys to a quiet place where we wouldn't be disturbed – the disabled toilet.

I still treasure that afternoon and when all is said and done I had shown myself I still had a bit of spark left in the old battery. Better still, I managed to sneak out with a couple of bottles of Domestos under my salwar.

But apart from my random encounters with men in motorway toilets, my proudest achievement on the Internet is setting up my knitting pattern swapping engine 'Knitster'. Of course I had some help with the web design, and some help with turning the computer on, but the idea is all mine. The concept is simple: if you have a knitting pattern you can store it on your hard drive and share it with others in the online knitting community. It strikes at the heart of the money-grabbing woollens industry with its massive profit margins and market monopoly. Knitwear is for everybody, man, so it should be freely available. But I was forced out of the market when my Knitmaster 2000 got a virus and started churning out peephole cardigans. Another victory for globalisation, another loss for the common older person.

Meeting people when you are a housewife

Madhuri Kumar

People are always telling me that being a 'homemaker' is a full-time job, but I can't say I've noticed. As far as I can see, when you're a housewife with just one adult child, waking up at 8am thinking of ways to fill the day ahead with no one to talk to can seem as impossible as swimming across a pitch-black bottomless black, black lake. So it's important to keep yourself busy by talking to as many people as you can. Here are a few ways of countering the unending loneliness of daily existence. I hope you enjoy them!

Spend a little bit too long in Asda

There's plenty to occupy you, just look at the salads. Or the pizzas. And most of all, ask one of the assistants to show you where things are. Some of them are very chatty and can really help lift your spirits with their brightly coloured uniforms and funny hats. One girl told me all about her boyfriend's receding gum problem while showing me the way to tinned goods. That really brightened my day. But remember, when you feel depression gnawing at the pit of your stomach, it's time for a treat: Marks and Spencer.

Flirt with a butcher

The many cuts of meat available at a butcher's provide practically limitless opportunities for innuendo and banter. And no butcher worth his salt is going to pass up an opportunity to flirt with all the housewives who come to admire his goods. But of course it doesn't have to be a butcher. You can also flirt very successfully with bakers and greengrocers. But under no circumstances flirt with a dry cleaner. I learned that lesson the hard way! All they want to talk about is lint and how to remove beetroot stains.

String along a cold caller

As long as you don't actually pass on any credit card details, pretending to be interested in buying something from a cold caller is an excellent way to fill an hour or two. The people on the phone have such jolly voices and ask such interesting questions like 'How long have you lived at this address?' or 'How many kilowatt units do you use in an average month?'. It's almost like a conversation I'd have with Ashwin. I don't know how often I've changed electricity supplier now, but on a slow day it can be up to three times.

Radio 2

Always have it on – it'll feel like there's a friend in the house. Jeremy Vine always talks about interesting issues, which could lead to lively debate. If you weren't sitting on your own staring at the carpet.

Neighbours

We live in a very friendly neighbourhood so I sometimes go for a cup of tea at the Aggarwals' house. Mrs Aggarwal is very nice and locks her Alsatian dog away before he tries to be 'friendly' with my leg, and we talk about our husbands and children. But I have to keep it a secret because Ashwin wouldn't like it if he knew I went there. He thinks Mr Aggarwal is a bit flash and they have a bigger house than us.

Drink

At about 3 o'clock your eyes might wander to the drinks cabinet. It's very important to avoid this temptation at least until Noel Edmonds' *Deal or No Deal* comes on.

Looking back at all of these suggestions I can't imagine why I feel so down a lot of the time. Many women of my generation would kill to have the life I lead. If you're one of those women, please feel free to use any of my tips. And remember: take each day as it comes.

Meeting people at college

Sanjeev Kumar

We live in a day and age and time when just about everyone has the opportunity to go into higher education. Obviously there has always been room in our universities for people with GCSEs in Maths, English and Woodwork. But it doesn't stop there; nowadays they're even letting in divs. But I ask myself, is that a good thing or bad thing? Is it right that Colin Dodd can get into college when he did nothing but eat chalk for five years, when I had to work very hard for a CSE pass in metalwork? Well I'm prepared to be generous and say all in all I think it's a good thing, because there are still standards. After all, I was one of the lucky few because I was fortunate enough to 'make the cut' and be admitted to one of the country's finest institutions for learning things – Slough Tech. I did a term there for my retakes. But I'm not going to start telling you about the long hours of revision I put in. Because I didn't. I was too hard for that. Instead I am going to tell you what college is really about – cutting loose and partying like there's no tomorrow.

Slough Tech was my first taste of independence from my parents (although I did go home at weekends). But when you leave home it's important to make friends fast. Luckily I have developed a few tricks to help you become massively popular in a student environment.

Offer to drive

If there's a party and you haven't been invited, offer to drive the popular people who have been invited. In fact, the difficult part of this is getting Dad to lend you the car in the first place, but I have a persuasive argument. I'm a grown-up man, I've tidied my room, and I'll go to the cash and carry on the way and pick up some stock for him.

So make sure there's room in the car for your party friends and some boxes. When you get to the party your popular friends sometimes let you in with them, but more often they don't. It is still a social coup, because you can say you've had girls in your car. And you can earn double cred points by hanging around outside and offering them a lift back at the end of the night.

Help Yourself with the Kumars

Be the centre of the fun

Learn to speak 'Vulcan' or learn some Monty Python sketches, which will keep your new friends entertained for hours and get the whole college talking about you. One of my proudest achievements was translating 'The Dead Parrot Sketch' into Vulcan and performing it in the college bar. By the end I was covered in beer and minor bruises. Throwing glasses of beer is the student way of saying 'You're one of the lads, now'.

Lend them your stuff

Buy lots of CDs and DVDs and lend them to people. They'll respect you for it and often talk to you when they apologise for breaking it – a great 'opener'. One of my deepest college friendships started when I lent Steve Cornish, who was in the year above, my leather jacket. Every time I saw him I'd say 'Alright, Steve, still wearing my jacket?' and he'd say 'What?' and pretend he didn't know who I was. That was what I loved about student life – the cheeky banter. I let him keep the jacket.

Develop your own sense of style

Clothing and fashion are important to students but individuality is the key. Just buying the latest jeans or top isn't going to impress this crowd. It's got to be unique. So on my first day at Tech I turned up in knee-length dungarees, ankle boots and topped it off with a pork pie hat. Mum helped with the sewing, but it was my own design and totally unique. You should have seen the looks I got!

Start a fraternity

The problem with British universities, compared to American ones, is there are no fraternities. We've all seen *Animal House* and *Teenage American Frat Party 3* – fine pieces of cinema. But not only are these good films, they also show you that fraternities are great fun. So why not do what I did? I pretended I was in a fraternity by borrowing one of Ummi's cardigans. Though I also had to pretend I'd been in a food fight on account of the tomato soup dribbles down the front.

The American fraternity look. Cool!

Get a nickname

All the most popular people at college have a nickname. Sometimes these are jokily rude about the person, like 'Beardy' or 'Knobby' which sounds insulting, but actually it means they've been accepted by the others and the mickey taking is of a friendly kind. I picked up quite a few friendly tag names while I was at college: 'Smelly', that was one, 'The Prat', that was another – remember this is all in jest – but my favourite was 'Bum-face'. The deeper the insult, the more 'in' you are.

Joining a clique

Once cliques and groups of friends have gelled at college it can be very difficult to break in, but one tried and tested method is to hover around at the edges saying things like 'Hey, are we up for fun?' and 'I heard there's a Star Trek Soc. disco tonight, are we going?' You see what I've done there? By using words like 'we' and talking about shared interests – Star Trek – I've joined the group without them even noticing it.

The canteen

The college canteen is at the centre of everything great about our educational institutions: subsidised food. I spent a lot of time in the canteen at college. A massive amount of time. Really enjoyed it. But I didn't make any friends there.

Join a club

One great way to meet people is to join a club or society. But remember that the best ones are always over-subscribed. I was turned down for membership of the debating club ... wine appreciation society, film club, the table tennis team, chess club, music club, the list is endless.

What was really surprising is that I was first in the queue for most of these clubs. That's how packed they are. But I did get lucky with one application: Star Trek Soc. From the moment I joined I knew this was it, I 'belonged'. There were a couple of disadvantages. Firstly, I had to play the female Star Trek officers and, secondly, they told me one of the rules was that the female officers had to buy all the beer whenever we went out. But my fondest memory of Slough Tech has got to be standing at the college bar, dressed as Lieutenant Uhura ordering ten pints of lager shandy. How cool was that?

Chapter two
Bringing friends home

How and when to invite friends into your home

Sanjeev Kumar

'Hello, will you come to my home and be my friend?'

What would you say to someone who came up to you outside Costcutter and said that? Well I can tell you, I used to get all kinds of responses. Most people walk a bit faster but sometimes you get lucky – like if a girl smiles at you, or once a bloke gave me a piece of his Crunchie bar and a pound coin. But no one actually ever came home or became my friend. Which is their loss, because I'm now on TV and they're not. Especially the man who shoved me to the ground and stole my jacket. Who's laughing now? It's me because I'm famous and it was a cheap jacket and I got a better one. But it was experiences like that, and the taunting I got from local schoolchildren, that made me decide to become famous. So those were the bad old days, before my genius was uncovered by me having a TV show broadcast to millions worldwide. If I stood outside Costcutter and asked the same question now, I'm pretty sure that there would be loads of takers and no one would steal my jacket.

But this raises an interesting question. How do YOU go about getting people to come round your house so your life can be as good as mine? I'm guessing you are not a well-known 'face' so you might be thinking 'maybe the Costcutter thing is a good idea and might work for me'. It won't. If I failed, you have no chance. Ditto for VG, Spar or any of the other franchises. But it's not the only tactic I tried in my pre-fame days. I had a number of ruses and some of them even worked. So here's my guide on how and when to invite someone to your home.

When

The question of when to issue an invitation to someone is one I've pondered many times. Definitely *before* you want them round, but how far before? There are two answers to this.

Firstly a long time before, like a year. This really gives them time to clear it with spouses and put it in the diary. Follow-up phone calls once a week should keep it fresh in their minds. Though you'd be surprised how often people still manage to forget.

Secondly, very shortly before, like a minute. 'Do you want to come to a party? Good, it's now.' This really doesn't give them any chance to wriggle out. Though I once invited a girl called Mandy Fisher to a party at my house using this technique. The problem was I hadn't had time to arrange a party. So she hung around for a bit and it was quite awkward. In the end she 'over-flushed' the upstairs toilet and Dad threw her out. Well, rules are rules. But if you invite someone to a party, make sure you're having one.

> *Sanjeev is having a barbecue on 10th July 2015. Please keep this date clear and bring something for the grill.*

This brings us to the most difficult part of inviting people round – the parents. They are always cramping your style, isn't it? There are times that I just want to chill with 'my crew' and 'hang with my posse' and the 'olds' are always having wine and cheese evenings. None of my 'homies' is going to put up with a bunch of boring old codgers eating cheese – though Sunil is quite partial to a bit of the old 'Danish blue' he always says. I know exactly what he's talking about, because I love strong cheeses myself. A bit of Roquefort spread onto some crusty bread, a couple of tomatoes – nice. Sometimes we sneak downstairs and feast on the Gouda but Dad always shouts at us and we have to go back to my room. Flipping heck! It's the same story every time. Whenever they have friends around for nibbles, I'm not allowed in the lounge, I'm not allowed to play my music, and there's no frying allowed because of the smell. It's like being in prison. Cheese prison.

The best time to get the lads round is mid-afternoon when Mum and Dad are out. Then at least I can pretend it's my own house – though I have to keep the noise down in case I wake Ummi.

Bad invitations

In an invitation avoid begging phrases like 'Please come to . . .', or 'I'm desperate for guests', or even 'I'll pay you to come'. These have never worked for me. Talk from a position of strength – 'The Sanjmeister commands you to attend his birthday party' is one I'll be using next year. If it is a birthday include a list of stuff you want as presents. This year I want loads of Pokemon stuff and any action DVDs – *Mission Impossible*, *X Men*, *The Hulk*. So please do come if you're in the area.

We've seen how to get people into your house the Sanjeev way. The next few bits of the book aren't written by me so you may want to flick forward to my next entry. It's up to you. But I really recommend it.

How to make your house welcoming

Madhuri Kumar

Hello, I'm Madhuri Kumar and welcome to my home. I'm delighted to present to you my tips on making your house pleasing to guests.

Imagine you've got some nice friends dropping over for a quick cup of tea, where do you start cleaning up? Well, I always begin with the first thing they'll see – the outside of the house. Start by giving the bricks a good scrub. This can take hours but makes a huge difference. Imagine how you'll feel when your guests turn up and say, 'Your bricks look nice.' You just know they're thinking about the filthy bricks they've got at home.

Dirty bricks.

Clean bricks.

Two topiaries close together can look like a bum.

A lot of women these days use industrial cleaning equipment, but I find a wire wool pad does the job.

When the roof is done, and you've cleaned the cement between the bricks, it's time for a quick look at the front garden. Uproot unwelcome or offensively shaped plants. Nothing gets things off to a worse start than a topiary shaped like a bum.

Then get on your hands and knees and scrub the pavement outside your house. Many women use high-pressure hose systems, but I find a wire wool pad does the job.

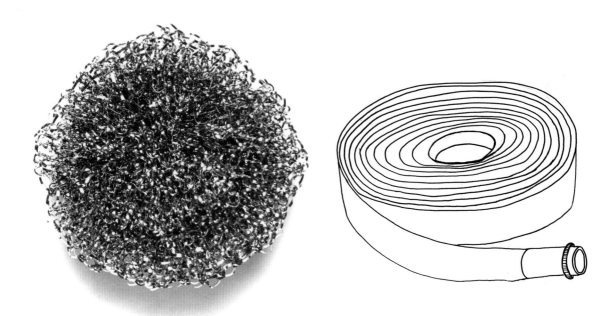

Who needs industrial cleaning equipment when a wire wool pad does the job?

Once the pavement is done we can move inside the house. You might be tempted to strip the wallpaper in the front hall. Don't worry about it. A couple of coats of brilliant white will suffice – it's only a cup of tea! Whereas if it's dinner with Richard and Judy, you might need to replaster the whole downstairs.

Make sure the house smells nice. Bad smells include fish, rubber, dog poo, petrol, tarmac and cigarette smoke. Good smells include air freshener, pot pourri, flowers and toothpaste.

You've done the basic groundwork, now it's time to get the house cleaned up.

Feng Shui – Chinese for tidying up

Thousands of years ago the Chinese invented tidying up and they called it Feng Shui. Before that, the old philosophers were always tripping over children's toys and discarded chopsticks. Then one day, the wife of the king said: 'I want this whole country tidied up.' And it was. Now the ancient art has come to England via India. Here are a few pointers to get your own house Feng Shui-ed.

Furniture

There are many complicated rules about how to arrange your furniture in the north eastern corner of your house, but I've lost the book, and anyway it's common sense. The lounge suite needs to face the TV. Dining chairs go around the dining table.

I recently revitalised our bedroom by repositioning the bed in the north western corner. The effect on our sex life has been electric, though Ashwin seems more interested by the fact that he can now see B&Q out of the window. Men!

Get any old boxes out of the way

Feng Shui is all about the flow of Chi in your house. So if your husband has left boxes of stuff lying around, get them out of the way.

Feng Shui says: This box is disturbing the flow of Chi in this room and could bring bad luck.

You see?

Houseplants

Having plants in the house promotes a feeling of well being.
But give careful thought to their positioning.

Right

Wrong

Make piles

Coffee tables are always getting covered in clutter, which can counteract Yang Chi and also look messy. *Feng Shui says*: Neatly stacking newspapers and magazines looks much tidier.

Kitchen

The kitchen is the soul of your house and must be kept clean at all times. Sometimes during cooking, pieces of food can end up on the floor or worktops. *Feng Shui says*: When you're done cooking, go round with a cloth or sponge and clean them up.

Lighting

I like to keep the curtains closed so robbers can't see what we're doing. While Ashwin always says: 'What does Feng Shui say about keeping the electricity bills down, eh? Does it have an answer to that? Does it?' It doesn't, so he keeps the lights off. We often sit in darkness when we have guests. It's fun to guess who they are by their voices!

Clothes

As soon as the laundry is done, put the clothes away. *Feng Shui says*: Folding clothes is a good way of fitting more into a drawer. Added benefit: they don't get creased!

Sleeping arrangements

If you have guests staying the night, make sure the spare room is uncluttered and free of mess. If your husband is anything like mine, the spare room will be full of excess warehouse stock and old receipts. *Feng Shui says*: Never sleep in a room where more than fifty toilet rolls are stored.

Thank you for reading this piece about making your house welcoming for your guests. If you've enjoyed it, why don't you read my other sections in this book?

DIY shortcuts
Ashwin Kumar

The second Madhuri tells me people are coming round, I panic. It's not that I dislike company, unless it's my neighbour Mr Aggarwal with his obsession that his house is bigger than ours. He has a slightly bigger hallway, that's all. Otherwise our houses are identical. But he can't resist commenting on how cramped our entrance hall appears and how he feels claustrophobic as soon as he steps through our front door. I really can't stand the man. Thankfully most of our guests don't make such vestibule-related comparisons. The reason for my disquiet is that there are always a few odd jobs that I've been putting off. Now is the time to tackle them. Starting with:

Tidy up your tools

The first thing any man guest in my house is going to get is a tour of my garage. I have all my tools laid out on a special rack with outlines drawn around them. This enables me to tell if they've been moved by as little as a quarter of an inch. If they have been moved I launch a full investigation. They don't just move themselves, do they? Someone must have been in there jumbling them all up and causing mayhem. Don't let anyone move your tools, it's the beginning of the end.

Man's best friend

Man's best friend used to be the dog but is now the cordless drill. I keep mine ready at all times – fully charged. But the cordless, be it a Black and Decker or Bosch or even the redoubtable DeWalt, isn't a toy, it's a powerful ally and a deadly enemy. When the chips are down and your back is to the wall you won't be reaching for an orbital sander or a mastic gun. No sir, because when it comes to combating household DIY problems, this baby is the only thing that stands between you and death. OK, not death, but certainly an inability to make holes. Actually, if you don't have a cordless drill a normal one will do fine.

Maybe I was a little presumptuous in my earlier estimation of the cordless drill as man's best friend. After all dogs can be trained to fetch, and to sniff out people after an earthquake. You can't do that with a cordless (not even the DeWalt!). So let's just say the jury's out. It may be that one day drill technology will replace the dog but not quite yet.

Dog vs. drill – the jury's out

Let's get to work

We've talked about tidying up your tools, we've talked about the best tools. Now let's get to work. Remember you're under pressure. In a few minutes Richard Madeley's going to arrive and if you haven't finished the job he'll stand over you and criticise the way you're doing it. This is to be avoided at all costs. No DIY man worth a bag of chipboard screws is going to let a daytime TV star tell him that he's using the wrong drill bit. So whatever the job, get it done fast.

The temptation
must be resisted.

Papering over the cracks

Papering over the cracks is an expression that's come to mean something bad, referring to an attempt to hide flaws or mistakes in a slipshod way. But this is totally at odds with the origin of the expression, which is literally to paper over the cracks. It's always a curiosity when the English language takes a twist like this. It's a quick, handy and cheap way to make a wall look good. Simply put paper over the cracks.

Wobbly tables

The number one irritation in a house is the old wobbly table. It's something we're all familiar with and I get a lot of letters asking me what a DIY-er can do about this simple-seeming problem. I've lost count of the number of times a wobbly table has caused undue irritation and disturbance at a social function. Unfortunately there's nothing you can do about it, so just stuff an old envelope under the shortest leg.

Make holes

The best pre-social DIY tasks involve making some holes in a wall. This allows you to use your cordless drill for what it does best. It could be part of a shelving project or hanging a painting or even putting in a kitchen unit. Once you've made the holes, tidy everything away and put your tools back. The outlines should help you remember where they go. When people come round make sure they see the holes and understand that you have ongoing DIY projects which you can talk about.

A final note of warning for the unwary DIY man: just as in ancient Greek legend sirens would lead unsuspecting mariners astray with their golden voices, there is a danger that lurks on the high seas of home maintenance – accidentally coming across the tool catalogue. Once opened the tool catalogue casts a magic spell over the reader. The promise of 'bulk buy' rawl-plug discounts and images of power tools can drive a man to distraction and he can slip into a hypnotic reverie lasting hours – only to be woken by the ring of the doorbell, the arrival of the guests and the sinking feeling of nothing achieved. If you come across the catalogue, just put it away in a drawer where it can't tempt you. Well that's my advice, you'd be well advised to take it.

Tips for being a good host

Sanjeev Kumar

Hiya and welcome. Did you see what I did there? As host of this page, I welcomed you into it. That's the sort of thing I'll be trying to teach you as you continue down the page. I do it without thinking because I am a naturally good host. But from the start, let me make one thing clear. You cannot learn to be a good host; it's inborn like being able to dance or fly an aeroplane. Dad's just told me that people can learn to fly aeroplanes but I think you get the idea – you can't just become a good host.

Dad's just told me that if I can't teach good hosting there's no point me writing this article and he'll get Ummi to write it. So I'm going to have to modify my earlier comment slightly. You can learn to be a good host.

The essence of good hosting is putting people at ease. When people come into your domain they may feel nervous so I like to start with a joke, which is easy for me because I'm a natural. I used to do a nice Monty Python sketch but my 'Dead Parrot' caused Aunty Bimla to swallow her dentures – it turned out her budgie had recently passed away. How was I to know? Anyway, the whole evening was ruined and I got the blame. So now I just do a quick 'Knock Knock' joke and leave the floor open to anyone else who wants to have a go. Hosting is a bit like being a comedy club compere, you've got to be the best, but you don't want to show anyone up. Keep it short and keep it clean.

Always be polite. Mind your P's and Q's. And your F's and B's as well. Because good hosts don't swear. If this presents a problem (like if you've got that syndrome which makes you swear) then say nothing. Unless that seems rude, in which case say something, but don't swear. Sometimes it may seem appropriate to swear, like if someone else has sworn, but don't be tempted. It's a trap and Dad'll come down on you like a ton of bricks. Remember, they can swear as much as they like, you can't. That's being polite.

Also, pay attention. If someone runs out of juice drink or cola, make sure you top them up. Same goes for biscuits or tea. If they have to ask you for anything, you've got it wrong. Great hosts like me have a sixth sense built in that tells us when someone is going to want something. Only last week I could tell that Aunty Bimla was going to be sick from too much juice, cola, biscuits and tea. Through my quick action and thoughtfulness I got her head out of the window before anything untoward happened to the carpet.

Know your way around your own house. People are going to need to know where the toilet is. The route to the loo should be marked out in your head so you don't fumble for words or get it wrong. I practise all the time. 'Up the stairs, follow the corridor, third door on your left' until it's smooth and unhurried. Never show uncertainty. The second you say 'I *think* it's the second door on the left', you've lost them. They lose all confidence in you and even become abusive. If this happens don't be tempted to retaliate (see above about swearing).

If your guests are staying to dinner you can give Mum a hand by showing them promptly to the dinner table. You can then show them how to dish out stuff onto their plates by doing so yourself. And then show them how to eat by eating. There are times when I've jumped the gun with this stage of the hosting process and started off without the others. But the situation can be redeemed by repeating the demonstration when they all catch up. At this juncture a note about belching. The rule about belching is very easy to remember – never before breakfast, always after tea. And it's polite to cover your mouth.

At the end of the evening your duties haven't finished. After dinner you might feel a bit kippy. It's tempting to just go to bed and let them sort themselves out, but that would be one of the classic errors of hosting. The host can't leave the scene of the crime until the guests have been shown out of it. However sleepy you are feeling, you have to put them first. My trick is to wait until dinner is over then start handing them their coats. This is the polite way of saying everyone's had a great time, now go home and let me go to bed.

These are the basics of good hosting, but like I said at the start it's not something you can learn. Except it is, otherwise I wouldn't be trying to teach it to you. I hope that's cleared everything up and there's no need for Ummi to butt in and write this piece again, Dad.

The way to your guest's heart is through their stomach
Madhuri Kumar

Reading the future with Indian snacks

Hello, Madhuri Kumar here again. And I'm delighted to introduce to you my own foolproof way of reading the future with Indian snacks. We're all inundated with kooky ways of predicting the future: horoscopes, crystal balls, tea leaves and treasury economic forecasts. (Ashwin told me to write that. He says it's satire.) Most have been dismissed as frauds by scientists – but not Snackology. This ancient technique for divining the future was invented by me a couple of years ago.

I had a friend who served her husband deep fried, sugary Indian *jalebi* three times a day on his favourite plate. Incredibly, he died at fifty. I took a good look at the plate and guess what colour it was? Yellow. In India, white is the colour of death. And yellow is almost like white. It seemed to me this was more than a coincidence. Could it be his fate was written in the snacks on his plate? This got me thinking about predicting the future with Indian snacks. You can learn a lot about people from how they handle their *gol guppas*. (Ummi told me to write that. She says it's innuendo.)

The rules of Snackology are very complicated and can only be truly understood through many hours of soul-searching and study. Or you can just look at this diagram.

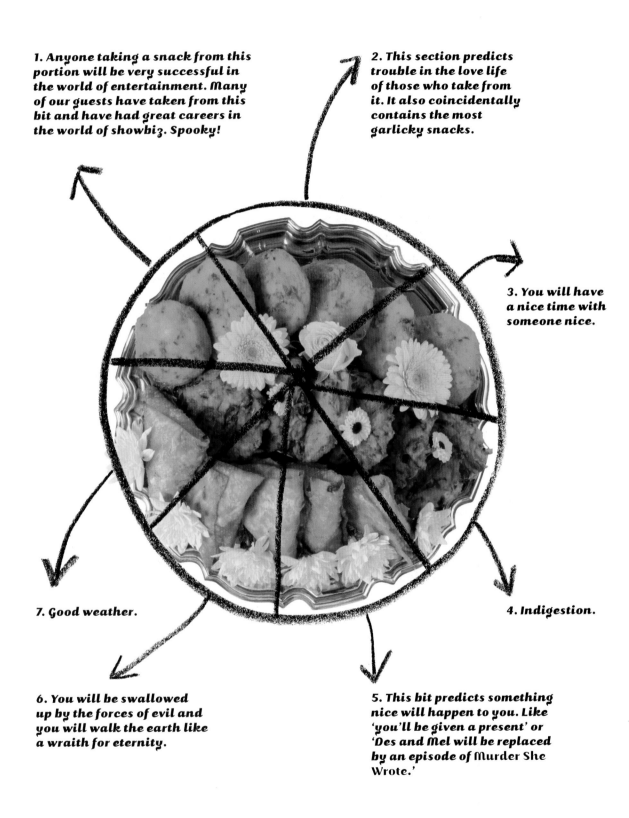

1. *Anyone taking a snack from this portion will be very successful in the world of entertainment. Many of our guests have taken from this bit and have had great careers in the world of showbiz. Spooky!*

2. *This section predicts trouble in the love life of those who take from it. It also coincidentally contains the most garlicky snacks.*

3. *You will have a nice time with someone nice.*

4. *Indigestion.*

5. *This bit predicts something nice will happen to you. Like 'you'll be given a present' or 'Des and Mel will be replaced by an episode of Murder She Wrote.'*

6. *You will be swallowed up by the forces of evil and you will walk the earth like a wraith for eternity.*

7. *Good weather.*

The power of Snackology was demonstrated to me time and time again when we had guests round.

Fern Britton taking a partially defrosted pakora, very unlucky – Fern was admitted to Middlesex General just hours later with a mystery illness.

Uh-oh! Lulu about to take an aloo tikki from the dark side of the plate – She was later caught stealing a statue from our house.

But it's not just our guests who prove the spooky power of Snackology.
Look at these!

Eisenhower takes a gol guppa with ludoos in the ascendant – the Allies went on to win the war in Europe.

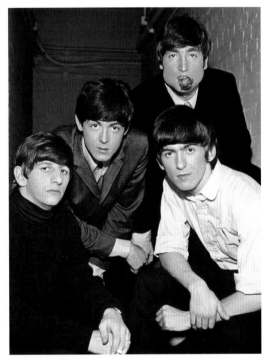

John Lennon takes a fateful onion bhaji when Ras Malai is in Pluto – John Lennon was assassinated some years later.

Can all of this be dismissed as merely coincidence or as Ashwin puts
it 'the ravings of one demented woman'? I think not, but the decision
is yours.

Make a meal of crackers
Madhuri Kumar

There was a time in the early eighties when things weren't going so well for us. It was a recession and Ashwin's business was going badly; we didn't have any money. A busy mother and wife had to make economies wherever she could. So when it came to dinner parties I needed something delicious but not too costly on the purse. I plumped for that old favourite, the cracker. Here's a recipe of mine for a formal occasion.

Crackers Provençale

INGREDIENTS
900g (2 lb) crackers
2 tablespoons crackers (crushed)
15g (1/2 oz) crackers
250 ml (8 fl oz) crackers mixed with water
2 crackers, beaten
25g (1 oz) freshly grated crackers
3 crackers (shredded)
1 small cracker (chopped)
1 teaspoon of dried cracker
pinch of cracker crumb to taste

FOR THE SAUCE
A pint of crackers, whipped
Fried crackers
450g (1 lb) crackers

GARNISH
Parsley

Combine all the ingredients together in a mixing bowl and bake for 1 hour in a fan assisted oven, at 200 C. The sauce should be warmed slowly in a saucepan taking care not to 'split' the crackers. If this happens, you have to start all over again.

A word about ingredients. If you can get them, the big name brand crackers are the best. Leave the packet out discreetly on display and it'll certainly raise eyebrows. But if you can't stretch to Jacob's or Carr's Table Water biscuits, I find most of the 'own label' brands are very good these days. Don't use Oatcakes – I save them for my Scotch broth.

Tackling celebrity spills and stains
Madhuri Kumar

If you have guests in your house, sooner or later they will knock something over or spill some ketchup. And let me tell you celebrities are no exception. The second a person gets even the slightest hint of fame, they seem to leave a trail of oil spots, hair sheddings and blood wherever they go. Ummi says we've got enough DNA on the lounge suite to start up CSI Wembley. The only two guests who didn't 'mess up' were Jane Seymour and Alice Cooper. Which surprised me too, the amount of perfume Jane's always spraying on herself you'd think she had B.O. but she doesn't. And Alice was a real sweetie – never once failed to use a coaster.

The most common mishap is sitting on a *pakora* or *bhaji*. It's easy for this kind of snack to slip off a plate and work its way under a guest star. But don't even think about trying to recover it until they stand up.

Now they're up and you can assess the damage. Is it still stuck to the person in question? If so a discreet flick with a tea towel should dislodge it and it will fall harmlessly to the floor where it can be dealt with. Sanjeev's a great help in this department, I've never known a *bhaji* to bounce twice. Emma Bunton's didn't even make it to the floor!

It's been my pleasure to get to grips with the waste products of a great number of top stars. Now, I'd like to share with you my top four celebrity messes and how I cleaned up. All of these have left a mark on both my memory and my furniture. I hope they will give you as much delight as they have me.

Madhuri's celebrity sofa stains

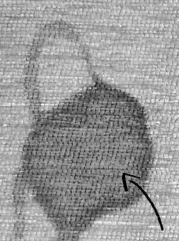

Number One: Ronnie Corbett and drink
I don't know if it was just nerves or celebrity clumsiness but Mr Corbett spilled his Tango all over the sofa. I was delighted and went at it with a patented mixture of detergent, soap powder and Windowlene. It didn't get the stain off, but it's a real talking point when people come round.

Number Two: The state of the toilet after Cliff Richard
I wouldn't want anyone to think all of my favourite clean-ups were restricted to the lounge. The 'smallest room' often has the biggest mess. But when I stepped into our W.C. after Mr Richard had 'been', nothing could have prepared me for what greeted my eyes. Yes! He'd spilled some liquid soap on the carpet and then tried to clean it up with some loo roll! He sent me flowers the very next day, but there was no need – the carpet's Flotex so it came out with a sponge and water.

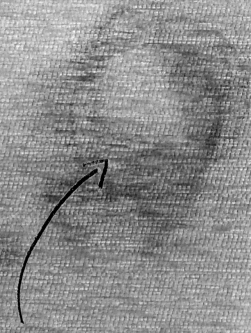

Number Four: Jam and Ray Winstone
Mr Winstone was one of our most charming guests – and always good to his mother. But where did he get all this jam from? He must have got one of those plastic packets from a motorway service station in his back pocket. Well, wherever it came from, it went off like a grenade when he sat down. But he was lovely about it, and jam is easy. Wait for it to form a crust, then use a paint scraper.

Number Three: Tracey Emin
An original wine stain by Tracey. Red wine is impossible to get out so I kept this one and called it an 'in-spill-action' piece.

Thank you for reading and if you've enjoyed these messes, why not make a few of your own and see how you get on with cleaning them up?

You are what you eat – what the rest of the family think

Dad
Lunch ideas

Import–export and warehousing is a demanding business. In the morning you could be dealing with the paperwork for a two thousand unit delivery of Turkish corn plasters. While in the afternoon you could be up to your neck in VAT receipts for a ton of Thai Tofu. That's why lunch is so important. Madhuri always packs me off with Cheese and Pickle sandwiches for my lunch. The crumbly yielding of the grated cheddar, contrasted against the firm tanginess of the pickle, provides a soothing and uplifting moment in a busy day. Try it with rye bread once in a while to liven things up.

Ummi
Get up and get going

The first thing I like to do in the mornings is wake up to my own Power Juice. Get some mango, prunes, broad beans, bran, Senokot and olive oil, and blend them all up to make my personal bowel buster. If that lot doesn't get things moving call a gastroenterologist; you've got serious problems!

The second thing I like to do in the mornings is give my gastroenterologist a quick bell . . .

Sanj
Energy snacks

I've got the sort of busy lifestyle that means I have to catch my meals on the go. Carrot sticks, pieces of celery, apples, cottage cheese are all things my fridge is well stocked with. Because I never touch them. Try to find any ham or pizza slices in there and you'd be out of luck. They don't last a second.

Topics of conversation

Holidays
Madhuri Kumar

Having people in your house is very nice, but it brings up a very special problem: what are you going to talk about? Conversations are very difficult and unpredictable things; they might start somewhere nice like talking about flowers and they could end up somewhere nasty like Ashwin calling Mr Aggarwal a communist because he's against flat rate taxation. To avoid tricky moments like this, I always ask my guests something both stimulating and soothing. Have they been anywhere nice on their holidays?

Now, the first response is crucial. If they say 'no' it could be terrible news – like they got sick on bad prawns or even that there was a death in the family and they had to cancel. So always be ready with some words of comfort like: 'What a shame, we went to Portugal and it was very nice.'

But if they say 'yes' to the question, they should follow up by telling you where they went. If they don't, it's polite to prompt them by asking 'Where did you go on your holiday?' Then when the ball's back in your court you should be ready with a lively response like: 'How lovely, we went to Portugal and it was very nice.'

Of course somebody else's idea of a nice holiday might be very different from yours. They might prefer trekking in the Andes or something like that. What a challenge! What a challenge it is to convince them that they've got it all wrong. I show them pictures of the Algarve or a mini break in Frankfurt to show them how much better it is. Then next time, they might go somewhere nice and have something interesting to talk about. I mean, there are plenty of fascinating things right on our doorsteps. Did you know that everyone in Europe drives on the right-hand side of the road? That's an interesting fact, and I bet they don't do that in the Andes.

But let's assume for a moment you are talking to people who share the same taste in holidays. The single most important thing to mention is all the lovely things you bought while you were away. Wherever I go I buy painted crockery, that's my special interest. I have a huge collection of saucers decorated with local scenes – which are always men fishing. When David Dickinson came on the show I asked him for a valuation and you know what he said? He said it would be impossible to put a price on them! He thought I shouldn't risk storing them on the walls where people could see them. So I put them safely away in a box in the attic.

David Dickinson has been to a lot of nice places.

Mostly 'nice holiday' conversations can last anything from minutes up to hours. But towards the end they can start flagging and turning to less pleasant subjects like flight delays or lost luggage. So when you feel this starting to happen, pretend you're burning something in the kitchen. Then when you come back into the room just say: 'We had an infinity pool and I couldn't keep Ashwin off the golf course' and the conversation should resume as normal.

The longest 'nice holiday' conversation I ever had was eight hours and thirty-two minutes. That was with Mrs Aggarwal who had been on one of the nicest holidays you could ever imagine – Portugal! Identical to us. That really was nice.

It's always nice to talk about your holidays.

You and your money
Ashwin Kumar

Opening up a conversation with a stranger is never easy. I've tried a number of conversational gambits over the years to captivate the guests who come to our home but nothing hits home more than money. Everyone has an opinion about money and you can be sure about that. In fact, I'd go so far as to say it's the king of conversational topics and can't be trumped – not even by an extension or a new garage.

Money is top trump.

So how to work money into the conversation? It's not always enough to just shout 'money!' and everyone starts talking about it – that's the kind of world we can only dream of at the present time. No, something more subtle is needed. Fortunately, there are any number of subjects which lead more naturally to cash. But I know that some of my readers may be a bit coy on the topic of readies. It is well known that many men would rather talk about embarrassing sexual problems than talk about their salaries.

If you are such a person I'd like to say I understand your problem. I'd like to say it, but I can't. I suggest that if you're a bit timid try talking about the price of your weekly shopping, and as you get more sure of yourself you can move up to interest rates, there's nothing for you to be ashamed about. But for the rest of us real men, the showman plunges straight in with tax returns or house prices. My finest hour was when I combined the two – taper relief on death duties for bequested properties. I was on fire that night! It was a shame our guests suddenly remembered they had to go to an evening funeral. I could have talked for hours.

But don't restrict yourself to just money. The broader world of economics is fascinating. I mean the last few decades have seen the rise of economic phenomena like YUPPIES (Young Upwardly Mobile People), TWINKIES (Two Incomes No Kids) and now SLOBBIES (Sanjeev Living Off Bloody Handouts). Do you have any idea what that boy has cost me? My advice is to classify live-at-home children as Stationery thereby making them tax deductible.

In 2003 I re-classified Sanjeev as a novelty staple remover – he's now 100% tax deductible

Ask yourself, do you have a financial strategy for an unplanned emergency? When Madhuri unexpectedly fell pregnant with Sanjeev I had to offload a lot of quality cookware at cost price to afford baby clothes. Don't get caught out – either plan ahead or don't be tempted by a weekend break in the European capital of romance: Didcot!

Perhaps I've drifted off the original point. Which is that money makes an interesting topic of conversation at any social gathering. I mean, what do world leaders talk about at all these summits? Global warming? I don't think so.

Interview techniques
Sanjeev Kumar

As I may have mentioned earlier, when I have a conversation with a friend, that friend is usually someone quite famous. And it's not so much a conversation as an interview. I spend a lot of time preparing for guests on my show, but all my questions are subjected to a critique before they can go on air. Sometimes the whole family have to work long into the night to get it right. Here's an example:

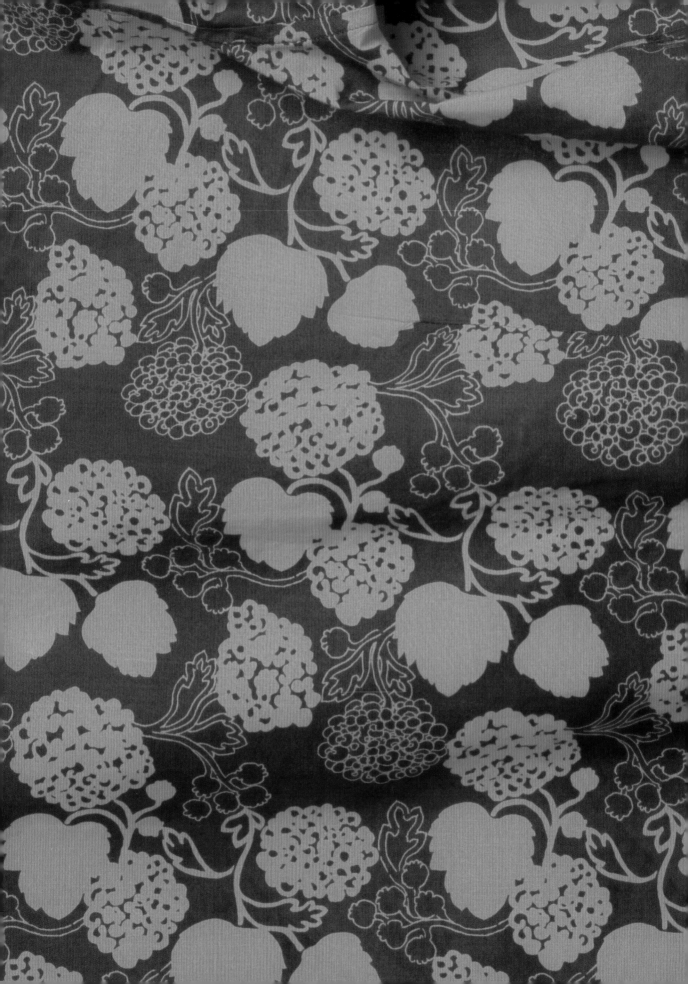

Chapter three
Spending time with friends and family

Mental agility and puzzles page

Ummi

As I grow older and more infirm, I notice with each year a decline in my physical strength. Soon I won't be able to stand properly or even goose passing men with the vigour I once did. But being old doesn't mean your brain has to die too. I'm more mentally nimble now than I was at the age of twenty, and let me tell you it was an age where my imagination ran riot. Well why not? I lived in a country where men wore skirts and coconut oil was in ready supply.

But to fight off the onset of senility one has to work hard. Some of the Wembley Asian Pensioners formed a pub quiz team a few years back. We called ourselves 'The Hip Replacements' and went to quiz night at the Dog and Duck. It all started promisingly enough; we did well in the first round in the quiz, which was luckily all about medical problems. But things went downhill in the pop music round and we lost heart. Me and my friend Asha started drinking rather heavily and heckling the question master, while Mr Das from the hairdresser's kept shouting out the answers. In fact the only one still taking it seriously was old Mr Bhatia, who remained stern-faced and quiet throughout. Sadly, it turned out that he had passed away during the Science and Technology round, which was a shame because that was his special topic and he would have scored well. So, perhaps inevitably, we were banned from the pub and that was that.

But I've developed a few armchair techniques to keep my mind supple over the years and I want to share with you some of my 'Mind Games':

Take three

It's a simple game. Imagine three things and weave a story out of them. Here's a starter to get you going: George Clooney, a dog leash and a tub of whipping cream. See? You're already thinking up a wonderful tale to take to bed with you.

So Don't Que

So Do Ku is a number puzzle invented by the Chinese. So Don't Que is a game invented by Indians. If you see a queue, barge into the front of it and pretend you only speak Urdu. It's a hoot at Argos.

Card games

These really are a fun way to keep your mind active – for instance, I'm always inventing new places to hide an ace or two. Unfortunately, the last time I played strip poker with Tom Jones he was showered in playing cards when I forfeited my negligée. Tom was a real gent though, he averted his gaze immediately. In fact, he left the room immediately. In fact, I haven't seen him since. Call me Tom. Please. I'm still 'holding a low pair', if you know what I mean!

Crosswords

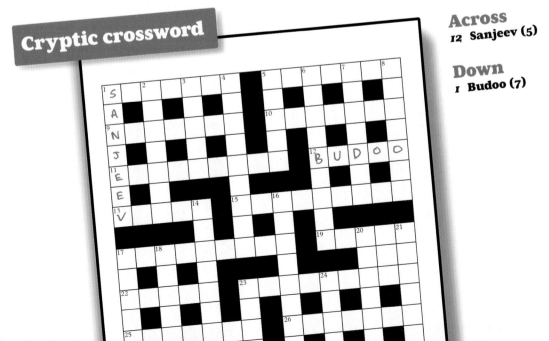

Cryptic crossword

Across
12 Sanjeev (5)

Down
1 Budoo (7)

Spot the difference

Mental fitness is all a question of observation. Test your observational skills by finding the differences between these pairs of pictures.

Easy

Ans: in picture two I'm wearing a bowler hat.

Medium

In picture two – trick question, no difference at all! Just joking, darlings. But the resemblance is uncanny, isn't it?

Fiendish

Should find four hundred and twenty-seven differences here.

Maths

A fat comedian tells a hundred jokes before he gets a laugh. If the comedian works for seven series on television and only gets two laughs, who is he? Ans. Sanjeev, who is also a Budoo.

Memory game

One of my tricks to beat off the inevitable onset of senility is to take a tray on which are placed twelve different objects. I take a quick look and then cover them in a cloth. Then I ask myself, what can I remember? Sadly very little. So I make myself think as hard as I can and try to stay focussed. Now, I do recollect a whistle. That reminds me of one of my first boyfriends, he was called Ravinder – he was a railway guard and he used to blow a whistle when it was time for the train to leave Jallundar station ... or was it Nabha? In fact he might have been called Jaspal and he ran a mango stall. No, that was Narinder. Still happy days. What was I doing? At this point I usually notice a tray covered in a cloth and wonder what it's doing there.

Wembley Pensioners' day trips

Or, Didn't we have a lovely time the day we went to Bognor?

Ummi

SATURDAY
August
12

August 12th 2006

I've had the most wonderful day of my life, all thanks to the Wembley Asian Pensioners' day trip to Bognor Regis. Or as Sharda and I call it: sand, sea, sari and sex! Yes, I pulled, and what a cracker! But the path of true love never runs true and this was to be no different.

SUNDAY
August
13

Let me start at the beginning, which was the coach trip. Me and the girls took the back seat and were messing around, throwing elastic knee supports at each other and trying to get Asha Kapoor's deaf aid to go into feedback mode, when I noticed a man I'd never seen before: tall, handsome, and with one good leg. I said to myself: 'Sushila, there's a man you'd like to tempt away from his day care worker.' So I went up to him and asked if he'd like any help adjusting his crutch. He laughed, so did his day care worker and we hit it off instantly!!!

Well, when the coach got to Bognor I had to get rid of the girls and the day carer somehow. Luckily there was an arcade with an old space invaders machine and Asha got stuck on level one so we sneaked off. Baldev, that's his name, took me for a promenade along the beach front. Well about ten yards of it, then he got tired and took a bench. But what he lacked in leg stamina he more than made up for in the tongue department. He polished off both our ice creams!

We talked and laughed so much I forgot myself, but luckily I had that card with my own name printed on it and it all came flooding back. Baldev bought me a balloon and he told me how lonely he'd been since he lost his wife, and I feel the same way since my husband passed on. Then we discovered some other things we have in common – bursitis, gout and we're both terrified of aneurisms. We even take the same yellow pills. By now I was thinking it must be fate that brought us together. But fate was going to tear us apart too.

We took off our shoes and took a walk on the beach and paddled. And as Baldev's crutch sank slowly into the wet sand I decided to throw caution to the wind and kiss him. But unknown to me the afternoon sun had warmed my balloon, and as I lunged it caught my hairpin and popped with an explosive bang. Well that put an end to the whole thing. What girl doesn't know the miserable feeling of riding home with her date in total silence, broken only by the siren and paramedics shouting for adrenalin. Embarrassed? I wished the ground would swallow me up.

Sanj's guide to Wembley

Sanjeev Kumar

Welcome to my world, my world of Wembley. This is my guide to what's going on in one of London's greatest bits. Wembley. The following information doesn't appear in any guide books or websites because you're getting it from a real insider. You could call it a Lonely Planet cum Rough Guide except it's not rough and I'm not lonely. That was a rumour started by Ummi, I actually have tons of mates. Let's stick to the point though: as a visitor to Wembley, if you want practical advice on what's on and what to do then read on. But like I said, don't expect me to show you around personally, because I have lots of famous friends to take up my time.

Transport

Wembley has the full range of transport, except ships. Cars, buses, trains, bicycles, even aeroplanes from Heathrow. So come to Wembley using one of these means of transport. If you are on a ship, change at London.

One of my friends.

Sights

Most people come to Wembley for one thing and one thing only. Footy-soccerball, the sport of kings. For the heart of Wembley is Wembley – the famous stadium where London United take on all comers in the National Football Division. So famous is Wembley that they're building it again. Tickets can be bought off the Internet (probably) and off blokes hanging around outside (definitely).

Sir Matt Busby-Berkeley leads London United to victory in the big cup with wings, which he later used in one of his musical extravaganzas.

Eating out

If you're in Wembley you'd be mad to leave without tasting the local food. Streetside cafés – called 'Kebab Houses' – cater for the discerning. And the not discerning. In fact if you're in there after eleven at night they cater even for the drunk. But this is all part of the charm of Wembley. And it's not just kebabs, there are some wonderful restaurants serving burgers and fried chicken. If you plump for one of these, go for the house bucket. Good value.

Two more of my many friends.

Top Ten Kebab Houses

Cheap

Costas – it's basic doner in here, no frills and also no napkins. Bring your own.

The Taste of Istanbul – the taste is pure Istanbul but the smell is actually of the drains. But if you can get beyond that, you're in for a treat. Medium kebab for under two pounds.

Mr Stavros – Mr Stavros is an institution. Sorry that should read, Mr Stavros is in an institution, sadly. But you'd have to be mad to sell taramasalata this cheap!

Medium price

Lucky House – this is actually a Chinese that's branched out into kebab preparation by popular request. Try the souvlakia with hoi sin sauce.

Bengal Palace – such is the demand for kebabs that this popular Indian eatery has also turned its hand to the Mediterranean delicacy. Be careful, it's three chillies hot. These guys put the fuse in fusion cookery.

Dazzle – probably the only gay kebab house in Wembley. My friends Tony and Peter run this eatery and always have a joke about which of them is going to prepare me my shish kebab. I tell them not to fight, they can both have a go. It usually takes a couple of skewers to satisfy me anyway. They've invited me out for a drink next week. Fantastic!

Stevie's Aussie Kebabie Placie – Stevie's a great bloke who moved here from Australia and now can't afford to go home. He's importing Ostrich burgers and selling them in kebabs from a hand cart. I promised I'd give him a mention.

Expensive

Nick's – if it's frou-frou tablecloths and modern lighting you're looking for, then look no further than the view from this restaurant. It's right opposite Habitat. Nick's makes the cut because it has a working lavatory (at time of writing).

Athens – this is Wembley's most romantic kebab house. The lights are low and there's nothing like a free extra dollop of mayonnaise to impress a date. The nook beside the fruit machine is very snug.

The Pomme d'Or – not strictly a kebab place but if you've got the money they'll almost certainly make you one.

Action sports

Soccerball may be the best known sport in Wembley, but radical board sports are on the rise. If you're looking for pure action, adrenalin and 'big air' come and watch me and Sunil skateboarding in the park – just past the swings.

Best time of year to visit

There are no bad times to visit Wembley. Conversely there are no good times to visit Wembley either. Come when it suits you, but don't expect to find me in.

I have mates.

Where to stay

Stay in a hotel. I have loads of mates staying at mine.

Ashwin Kumar's guide to skips

Ashwin Kumar

When I first came to London, it wasn't the Houses of Parliament or the GPO Tower that caught my eye. It was the many bright yellow skips of the Goldhawk Road and surrounding environs. To a young man like myself they were a world of opportunity and adventure. Nothing made me happier than a day spent rummaging through a load of discarded soil, or returning by cover of night to dispose of an old carpet. Then came marriage and that side of my life simply had to go. Madhuri always resented my love of the 'yellow goddess' – she said I would have married a skip if I could have. I'm not sure that's true but I certainly sowed my wild oats among them. Crazy days. But now Sanjeev's grown up and Madhuri spends her afternoons watching *Inspector Wexford*, I've recently taken the opportunity to return to my old haunts and I can tell you that today's London skips are more impressive than ever.

Where to find skips

Skips are to be found just about anywhere. Builders' yards, houses where they are clearing stuff out and of course at the skip depot. The depot is no use to the skip scavenger, because all the rubbish has been removed. But for the purist, it's *the* place to go to see a lot of skips in one place – the lines unsullied by distracting rubble and refuse. Also the depot is an ideal place to monitor the comings and goings of skips; you can follow the lorries to their destinations, then add each location to your skip position master planner.

This helps you keep track of which skip is where. You don't want to 'double visit'. There's nothing more frustrating than sifting through a skip only to realise you've been there before and had all the good stuff.

Skip-I-quette

To the casual observer, it might seem that skips are a free for all. But this is not the case. A complex set of rules govern skip usage which I call 'skipiquette'. Humans are social animals and people who hang around skips are no exception. The unspoken rules guiding who takes what, and in what order are a subtle language which is never spoken or written down. It's a lore held in secret by all us skip men. You would never understand it anyway, unless you were involved in the removal of items from a skip over a long period of time. Even if I could explain it, it would take me a thousand years. But basically it's 'first come, first serve'.

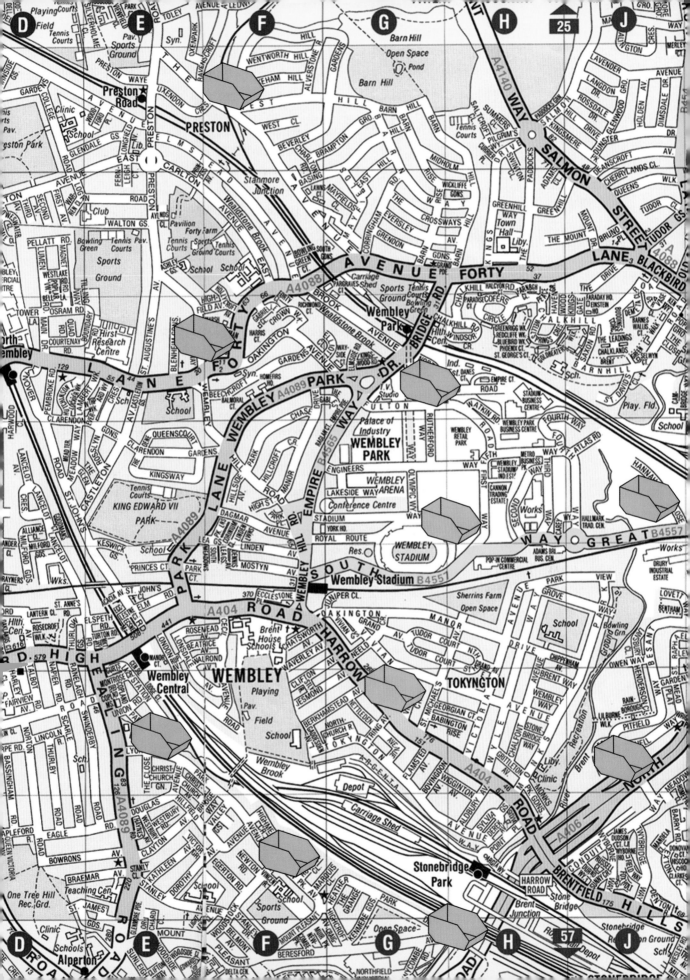

The anatomy of a skip

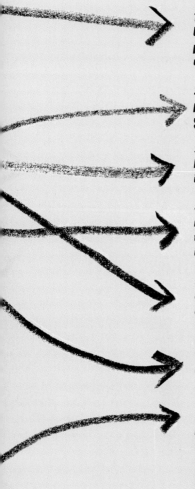

1. A broken washing machine – if you're after powerful magnets at low, low prices, i.e. nothing, then you've struck gold. And the motor parts must surely be useful for something. Store them in your garage until you find out what they are.

2. Splintered bit of old wood – wood has a thousand uses. And this piece of wood is also peppered with free nails and screws. Store in your garage.

3. Rubble – laying a drive or building a patio? Then you'll need some hardcore as a basis for the tarmac or paving surface. If such a project is a way off as yet, simply store in your garage.

4. Garden waste – the skippers' bane. All it does is disguise what might be hidden underneath and is of no use to anyone. On second thoughts free soil might come in handy one day – bag it and store in your garage.

5. Old shelving – though it might be broken and full of woodworm, old shelving can be made as good as new with a great deal of work and time. Store in the garage until you have time for this project.

6. Metal – skips often contain bent and twisted pieces of metal which are very heavy and sharp but have no use. So be careful as you remove these pieces to store in your garage.

7. Computer – look at that! Someone has thrown out an old computer. The hard drive will contain thousands of their personal files and perhaps details of their commercial transactions. It may even belong to a business rival and the information encoded on the hard drive could give you vital knowledge about their dealings. True, the computer looks severely damaged by rubble and is full of rainwater, so you might think it's beyond hope. But you are forgetting the steady march of technology which will one day make it possible to read a hard drive that's been shattered to pieces then immersed in mud. Take it home and store in the garage until such a day comes.

As you can see, the world of skips presents an opportunity for adventure and interest greater than any other I know. And I include chartered accountancy in that statement! All you need to succeed is an eye for free stuff, a pair of sturdy gloves and a garage to put it all in. Happy skipping! Oh, and put a bit of old sackcloth down in the boot of the car to avoid damaging the carpet.

Girlfriend, take control of your life! – by dutifully following your husband who is your god

Madhuri Kumar

Hello, Madhuri here once again, with an item for the ladies. If your husband's reading this with you, tell him to look away now. We don't want him finding out all our ladies' secrets, do we? Now, I'd like to share my own radical feminist advice to young brides on how to best please your husbands.

First let me tell you about my mother. She was the first feminist in her village. When she heard about women chaining themselves to railings to get the vote she joined them in her own protest. She chained herself to her kitchen sink. Father helped her, because he was very behind the cause of women's liberation too. And, as it was a long protest, she whiled away the time by doing the washing up. Being brought up in such a radical household it won't surprise you that I too practise strident feminism, when Ashwin lets me.

When I got married, Ashwin must have thought I was going to be like any other Indian bride – a complete pushover. But I soon put him straight on a few things. I told him in no uncertain terms that the kitchen was to be my domain, as was carpet cleaning and laundry. If he didn't like it he could just go out, get a job and bring home the bacon. Then I averted my eyes, ironed his trousers and made him a cup of tea. He seemed genuinely pleased with our 'equality' and I'd made a bold step on the road to women's liberation.

Of course, a lot has changed since those days. Girls now have tattoos and body piercings – but men and women will always be from different planets. Men like cars and DIY and being in charge, women like being treated to dinner and agreeing with their husbands. Stop me if I'm shocking you, but that's feminism. So if you are a young bride here are my ground rules for being a feminist:

1. Be assertive – there's no substitute for tackling household grime in an assertive way.
2. No means no – if your husband says no to you buying a new dress or some make-up – he means it.
3. Never let a man speak over you – instead stop talking altogether as soon as he opens his mouth.
4. Leave behind all those outmoded concepts – remember all those comedies in the sixties and seventies about the husband going out to work and the wife being there to cook dinner when he came home with the boss? Well these days, the wife expects a bit more than a peck on the cheek. Chocolate or flowers would do the trick.

I hope you've enjoyed my political discussion on the subject of women's liberation and I hope I have not offended any men. Thank you so much for reading. MK.

Father and son

Ashwin Kumar

In this day and age, with divorce on the increase and families fragmenting, bonding between parents and children is an increasing struggle. Which is no great shame – I don't think I'd want to get into team hugs and sharing-our-true-feelings-for-one-another kind of territory with Sanjeev. I have golfing partners I'd rather do that with. I don't think I'll ever forget the day that I bogied on the ninth and then told Bruce Forsyth about the tough time I'd been going through at the warehouse. We talked in an open and manly way and somehow everything seemed alright again. But it's the sort of experience I would never dream of sharing with Sanjeev. The thought of it makes me shudder, I mean what if he told me he loved me? I'd rather hear that from Bruce Forsyth, and I'm not too keen on hearing it from him.

I remember when Sanjeev was little he would always be pestering me to do something with him, so I eventually agreed. We did my accounts together – a privilege for a seven-year-old boy, you would think. But we had hardly got started before he was saying he was bored and wanted to watch TV. So it's not my fault that I can't communicate with the boy.

As you can see, this leaves me with a great problem that affects all men who have children. How do you show them the love and encouragement they need to become useful and productive human beings while keeping them at arm's length?

Well, there is one way of spending quality time with your son that has been preserved in the Asian community. The noble passing on of manual skills that have been handed down through generations – I'm talking about the assembly of flat-pack furniture.

Read the plans thoroughly.

All father-son teams go through 'the shouting stage'.

And the crying stage.

Eventually, everyone finds their rightful place.

My TV friends

Madhuri Kumar

Watching TV has been a great support to me over the years; in fact some of the faces I watch on the box every day have become like close personal friends.

I watch a broad variety of programmes ranging from the afternoon repeats of *Inspector Morse* through to the afternoon repeats of *Inspector Wexford* and all points in between. And each one of them is like a real friend (or bitter enemy in the case of *Rosemary and Thyme*). So before they come on, I always go through the ritual of tidying the front room and getting a pot of tea and a plate of almond slices ready as if a real guest is coming to see me. It's very exciting.

Wexford

Mr Wexford is my favourite detective of all time. He's tall and manly, a little gruff at times, but all that belies a shy charm and a great love of culture. You wouldn't think a West Country policeman would know so much about paintings and architecture, but he does which is a pleasant surprise. He also has old-school manners and a big red face, which I also find very appealing. There should be more detectives with florid complexions, broadcasters please take note. I think Wexford would be the ideal friend. Courteous, understanding, but with a volcanic passion just waiting to erupt. Ashwin can't stand him – I think he's a little jealous!

Red-faced and well-mannered – the ideal friend.

Sherlock Holmes

Sherlock Holmes is a classic but I'm not sure I would describe him as a friend. Dr Watson would be a better guest, always getting things wrong in an amusing way, but he's very loyal and always there to back Sherlock up with his revolver. I think Sherlock himself might be a bit too clever, and Jeremy Brett gives me the willies.

Wycliffe

Beautiful scenery.

Rosemary and Thyme

This is the one show that really gets my goat. Felicity Kendall was truly lovely when we had her on the show, but this can't really be described as her best work, can it? I mean how many times can you realistically find a body while raking some leaves in the garden? Two, three at the most. And who thought up the names? Rosemary is a perfectly 'herby' first name, but Thyme isn't. I don't know anyone called Thyme, do you? They had to get round it by making it a second name. It drives me to utter distraction, and sometimes I eat the whole plate of almond slices before the end. So I feel angry and sick. But they do film in some lovely gardens.

Poirot

David Suchet is such a charmer that you can forgive the very obvious padding to make him look fat. I like to imagine that if Poirot came round he would bring some lovely Belgian chocolates, which I adore. But he would be a bit strange, always checking his moustache in the mirror and flicking specks of dust from his jacket. I would always be worrying that the house wasn't clean enough for him.

Inspector Lynley

He's very posh, isn't he? I'm not sure someone this posh should be solving murders, but he would be nice to have round for a cup of tea. So tall and handsome, I think I'd be a bit giggly!

Those are just a few of my TV friends. Perhaps you can make some TV friends too. It's very easy, just turn on the TV and imagine that the murders and funny bits are all going on in your living room. You'll soon find you're talking out loud to the characters and joining in their lives. But please make sure you stop before any members of the family get back home.

Chapter four
How to be a good friend

How to help friends in need

Ashwin Kumar

Hello, Ashwin Kumar here with another piece of helpful prose to delight you. I like to think of myself as a helpful man and I look for any opportunity to do what I can to assist those I know. So much so, that among my colleagues at the Asian Business Association I'm known as rather a Good Samaritan and even a bit of a liberal. When we recently had a debate about the European Court of Human Rights with its rulings on minimum wages and overtime restrictions, I was one of the few people who stopped short of calling for a complete destruction of the European Union and Brussels. Admittedly, I stopped only a little short of it, but my gesture was enough to earn me the reputation of being a bit of a softy. Ever since then many people have come to me when they need a shoulder to cry on. So I've started a small charitable organisation called 'Ashwin's Friends in Need'.

Ashwin's friends in need

Let me tell you about some of the people I've been helping recently. When my friends found out that we were writing a book, they came to me with their tales of woe. Take the case of Mr Dhaliwal of Dhaliwal Motors, Wembley. He was in a terribly low state when he came to me and said: 'Ashwin, I'm miserable, can you help me?' I said: 'But how Mr Dhaliwal of Dhaliwal Motors, Wembley?' And you know what he said? He said: 'I'm miserable because I've got a yard full of top-class, second-hand commercial vehicles. Yet, demand is so low that I've had to slash prices in half.' Well that's a very sorry story, so I asked him to remind me of his current address. He said: 'Right on Wembley High Street, just past the Bengal House take-away. You can't miss us.' And I said: 'You mean like in your adverts?'

'I mean exactly like my adverts. Top-class, second-hand commercial vehicles with a one-year warranty,' he retorted. I'm glad to have given him the chance to get that off his chest.

I've remembered another story. Recently, a very good friend of mine was stuck with a very large number of DVD recorders that had no

import licence. He came to me and asked what could be done. With no licence he couldn't legally sell them. I scratched my head in vain. There didn't seem to be a solution to this one – I'm still working on it. Let's hope I come up with something before they get stolen, I joked. I mean they are stored in a secure lock-up on 37 Hanborough Road, Pinner. But what if someone should find out that the door opens if you rattle the catch? Well, my friend would lose it all and have to claim on the insurance. 37 Hanborough Road, Pinner. Rattle the catch. Let's hope no one does.

And it's not just friends I try to help. This is a story sent in along with a donation towards the running of this book.

'My name is Dave, I recently moved to this area and didn't know anyone. But within days of joining Wembley Connections I had met hundreds of nice looking young women for friendship and fun. Wembley Connections really know their business when it comes to finding a partner. Thanks, Ashwin, for giving me the chance to tell this true story in your book.'

Well that was heartwarming. These are just a few of 'Ashwin's Friends in Need' that I've managed to help. But there were so many that I simply wasn't able to do anything for, because they forgot to enclose a cheque to cover the administration fee. But it feels good when you help people and I'd like to help as many people as I can. Perhaps you are having trouble in your business life or just need someone to help you by listening and then publishing your story. Well now you know that you can always turn to Ashwin Kumar when times are difficult. Always remember to enclose a cheque for twenty pounds with your stories for the second edition of this book. It covers the running costs associated with publication. And if you have any advertisements that would help illustrate your story they can be added at a nominal fee of five pounds per square inch. For an additional consideration your tale of woe can be included in my upcoming pamphlet: 'Ashwin's Christmas Friends in Need'. Please remember that 'Ashwin's Friends in Need' is a registered charity so is not liable for UK tax.

The Kumars' guest contract

Ashwin Kumar

Many people have commented on the lavish hospitality we show our guests when they come to be on the show. But the first question they ask is: 'What's the legal and contractual basis for all this hospitality?' Well, we have a standard contract drafted by myself to avoid expensive legal overheads. Who needs big-shot lawyers who charge through the nose? I knocked this up on a word processor and had my old friend Mr Chaudry take a look at it. He was disbarred for fraud so he knows all the loopholes. I have to say I'm rather pleased with it and I've reproduced it in full so you too can enjoy it.

Contract

The Kumars at No. 42

DEFINITIONS

Heretofore you will be known as the 'guest' and the Kumars family will be known as the 'hosts'. Unless otherwise stated.

'Parties' refers to people not 'parties' – which have been banned until Sanjeev pays for the damage to the living room carpet.

FEES

The hosts (that's us) agree to pay the guest (you) the fee. To wit one 12 oz jar of Bimla's chutney.

The chutney shall be rendered unto the parties of the guest once their obligations as outlined below are done. How they split the jar with their agent is up to them, but 10% is usual I understand.

No equivalent cash value for the fee (the chutney) is available but they have been known to sell at a mark-up on eBay.

GUEST OBLIGATIONS

1. The guest shall confine himself or herself to the communal areas of the house. Male guests are forbidden from entering Ummi's bedroom. This is for their own safety.

2. Female guests are forbidden to touch Sanjeev. This is for his own safety. If, however, you do touch him, you may be obliged to marry him.

3. While we're on the subject of touching, don't go anywhere near the shelves in the living room. They're a bit dodgy and I'm sick and tired of having to prop them up again just because the likes of Phillip Schofield pop their gin and tonic down for a second. Is there something wrong with using the table?

4. Guests are expected to talk when asked a question. Failure to talk contravenes the whole point of the guest being there.

5. Guests are expected to listen while the question is being asked.

6. Rambling. We don't want the sort of guest who yarns on and on about some old subject, never finishing one story before moving on to another. It reminds me of my old friend Mr Khan. He would always start talking about his friends and acquaintances in the middle of a completely different topic of conversation. Picking out some eccentricity in their character and making a long pointless tale about the whole thing and all the time you'd be thinking 'Get to the point, what are you trying to say?' One time he went off on a digression lasting some minutes during an Asian Business Club dinner speech. So I started talking to someone else. Mr Stanway – he organises the catering. And he'd done a particularly good job with the

sandwiches which deserved a mention. But Stanway has a nervous tic which looks like a wink. So whenever I said something like 'Where did you get this fish paste, Mr Stanway?' he'd wink and say 'Only from the finest suppliers, Mr Kumar.' It was very funny. So, don't ramble.

7. The guest will use the coasters. Madhuri asked me to put this in but it follows on from Rule number three. The table's made for putting your drinks on and so are the coasters. Don't think you can pop your glass on the arm of the sofa or armchair, willy nilly, whenever it suits you. Would you do that at home? I don't think so, Mr Hot Shot.

8. Please flush the downstairs WC with a follow through motion. Failure to do so may result in a floating rights issue.

EXPLOITATION

The hosts shall have sole charge and control over use of the contribution made by the guest. Including the use of pictures on advertising for third parties.

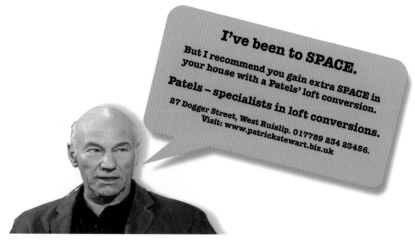

I've been to SPACE.
But I recommend you gain extra SPACE in your house with a Patels' loft conversion.
Patels – specialists in loft conversions.
27 Dogger Street, West Ruislip. 017789 234 23456.
Visit: www.patrickstewart.biz.uk

The hosts also have sole charge and control over use of the guest's name in web domains on behalf of third parties.

ASSIGNMENT AND LICENCE OF RIGHTS

The guest hereby agrees:

To waive all moral rights or rights of a similar nature in regards to the production and eating of snacks on the programme. The guest shall not mention any proprietary snacks belonging to any company other than Bimla's, Aunty Bimla's or any subsidiary of Ashwin Kumar Enterprises without prior arrangement.

To waive all moral rights or rights of a similar nature to any amusing anecdotes developed during the course of the interview such as stories about business acquaintances, road directions or events in the 1960s that may have happened to Ashwin and Madhuri Kumar. These are the sole property of Ashwin and Madhuri Kumar.

To waive all moral rights or rights of a similar nature to any interesting new kinds of sandwich invented during the course of the interview. Under the Copyright, Designs and Patents Act (1988) these are the sole property of Sanjeev Kumar.

To waive all moral rights or rights of a similar nature to any filthy innuendo involving the guest and Mrs Sushila 'Ummi' Kumar. Such innuendoes are her sole property and she reserves the right to use them in her fantasies without prior consent.

Signed by or on behalf of
The hosts

Signed by or on behalf of
The guest

You would think an agreement like this would be comprehensive in all respects. But celebrity guests always want to add their own 'riders' to the contract. Some demand their own dressing room or some such thing, but there were a few interesting ones. Frankie Dettori wanted to ride a horse into the studio, which I had to turn down for insurance reasons. But I pride myself on my flexibility, so I offered him a piggy-back on Ummi from the lounge to the interview. In the event, he declined but right up to the last minute I had my mother wearing a bridle and stirrups ready to honour the contract.

George Hamilton insisted that he had to have a sensual warm oil massage before the show. Ummi to the rescue, again. She had him laid out on the ping-pong table in the garage for almost two hours. I wouldn't have minded but they used two litres of my Castrol GTX which Mr Hamilton never paid for!

Probably the strangest request we had was from Tracey Emin. She insisted that Sanjeev was locked in a wardrobe while the rest of us threw over-ripe casaba melons at it and shouted abuse at the top of our voices. When I asked if this was one of her installation pieces she said mysteriously: 'No, it's just something I've been wanting to do for a long time'. Well, I refused point blank. Does she think I'm made of melons?

My celebrity friends

Sanjeev Kumar

I have a very large number of friends and dividing my time between them is a difficult balance. So what I do is I split them into groups or categories for easy indexing. The first group is composed entirely of people I knew before I was famous. So Mum, Dad, Ummi and Sunil. Though I have to say, before I had my show Sunil used to ignore me in the street and when he did talk to me he thought my name was Bunty. But that's showbiz – you only find out who your real friends are after you're famous. And Sunil made the effort to learn my real name and be my mate. But now I've reached the place which I have reached, I have another group or category of friends which are the ones I've met after becoming famous. People often ask me if I prefer the famous ones to the non-famous ones, which is a stupid thing to ask. Of course I do, they're famous like me. The question is how to divide the time between the two. And given a choice between going to the park with Sunil or going to the park with Charles Dance, it's the Dance-meister every time. The only problem is that Sunil is usually down there anyway, and you have to let him join in or he sulks.

Anyway, Sunil usually cheers up if I give him a go on my bike. Which is where I got the idea of offering celebrities a go on my bike. It's really a very quick way of gaining intimacy and doing something really nice for someone.

But the problem with my (famous) friends is that they can be very forgetful or just very busy or just very unfortunate. I know for a fact that Tom Jones was really looking forward to a cycle round the precinct but he remembered at the last minute to go to a concert that he was performing in but had forgotten about. Close call and lucky he remembered.

Natasha Kaplinsky was the only one who took me up on the bike ride and she really took off like a bat out of hell. I followed her on my racer for a couple of miles before I fell foul of the old asthma, so took a breather in Kentucky. But by the time I'd re-saddled the trail had gone cold. So if you're reading this Natasha, thanks for being on the show, and is there any chance I can have my mountain bike back?

But don't feel you have to lend someone your bike to get on the right side of them and show them what a great bloke you are. There are loads of ways of just spending a bit of time with them.

Take the case of Gordon Ramsay. I took him down to the park for a game of rounders. He's quite a good bat, actually, and after a couple of goes he whacked the ball onto the main road. I was dodging traffic for ages to get my tennis ball back and when I returned to the pitch, Gordon had gone. I suppose he just ran round and round until he had about a hundred rounders and figured it was game over. Gordon, how about a re-match?

David Hasselhoff was another one. He went to get some chips but never came back. To this day I don't know what happened to my large portion with a battered sausage. Hof, give me a call – you can keep the fiver.

I've also exchanged emails with a couple of celebs, to see if we can meet up.

	New Message
Send Chat Attach Address Fonts Colors Save As Draft	

To: Sanjeev Kumar <specialsanj@kumarsnet.co.uk

Cc:

From: Ronnie Corbett

Subject: Re: Do you want to go out sometime?

Signature: None

Hello Sanjeev,
It was very nice to be on your show and meet your charming family. In reply to your question about meeting up for a drink or something, I'd be only too delighted. I think I might have an opening some time in 2008. I'll contact you nearer the time.
Yours truly,
Ronnie

Is that a result or what? My diary is really filling up. Though there have been some tragic replies. For instance, Jools Holland's agent phoned to say Jools had been committed to a mental asylum until further notice and would not be able to come to the pub as arranged. Apparently, if you see him on the telly it's his twin brother who is also called Jools.

What a shame that Jools' career has come to an end in this terrible way. And let's wish new Jools every success for the future. It's amazing really how many tragedies like this have happened to people who've been on the show. I've had replies to invitations that would turn your hair grey.

Like, I rang Melinda Messenger to see if she wanted to take in a movie and her sister told me she'd been kidnapped by Mexican banditos. I even called June Whitfield to see if she fancied a sherry and a kebab but her lodger said she had been swallowed by a whale on a beach holiday. It's incredible that it didn't make it into the newspapers. Well, I'll sign off – I'm meeting Alan Alda for a bit of shopping down town – he knows the best brand of medicated talc for my sweat rash. He says he'll be disguised as one of the perfume girls in Boots. I guess I'll just have to ask them which one is Alan Alda. What a joker!

How your friends can help you

Ashwin Kumar

'No man is an island,' wrote John Donne. He had a point, but I do
sometimes find myself taking a bath and wondering what it would be
like if I was an island. My arms and legs would be peninsulas, my chest
a thickly wooded forest, and boats from many countries would dock
around my belly – bringing news and goods from all over the world. Ah,
would that it were so. You see we all like to think of ourselves as totally
self-sufficient and independent. But could we really survive without the
support network of loved ones we've built up around us? I would not
want to be without my beloved Asian Business Association. Who else
would I turn to when I need a tip on the stock market or a parking
conviction quashed?

One of the most difficult things to do in life is to ask for help. A man
and a woman lost driving in a city. The man poring over a map, the
woman tearing her hair out because he won't ask for directions. It's
a familiar scene. And yet why doesn't the man ask for help? Probably
because he thinks he can work it out in a minute. And would they be lost
anyway, without his wife's incessant interruptions about how so-and-so
is having a hysterectomy? Then he's got a son and mother on the back
seat, calling each other names. Debts piling up and the bloody
government's increased corporation tax. And now he's got to go on his
bended knee to some stranger to find out which turning he's missed.
Well I'm not doing it. I'll talk to the map – at least it doesn't change
its mind every ten minutes about which side of the North Circular
we're on!

So it's quite natural not to seek help. I want you to see your friends as
more than just people who you see from time to time for a glass of wine
or dinner. Think back to my thickly forested chest hair on 'Ashwin
Island'. Imagine that life is just such a jungle and you are Tarzan. Your
friends are the vines that you swing from tree to tree on. Now, clearly
your wife is Jane but your remaining family have to play the part of
the chimp. No analogy is perfect.

But how, you ask, will your friends help you tame this jungle so your
wife and chimp cum family can walk its paths and swim in its lagoons
safely? Well let's say the jungle is threatened by a rogue elephant – the

equivalent of a deranged bank manager. This rogue elephant is running around trampling, smashing and foreclosing on property loans without recourse to credit history! It's a terrifying idea.

Jane hugs you for protection, your chimp/family jumps up and down going 'Ooh, ooh, ooh'. What does Tarzan do? He uses his human cunning. Rather than a head-on fight with an elephant, he befriends the tiniest creature in the jungle, the bee – the equivalent of an independent financial advisor. These IFAs on their own are not very frightening, but when they swarm they can cause havoc. On your signal they attack, stinging the rogue elephant into submission with their combined reports to his head office.

Now the jungle is safe once more. You can take Jane out for dinner and your chimp can eat as many nuts as it wants – the equivalent of Sanjeev and Ummi eating as many nuts as they want.

Well I think that little analogy clearly demonstrates how important it is to turn to your friends when you're in need. If only all things in life were as neat and simple to explain as this.

Me Tarzan, you Jane, Sanjeev and Ummi are chimps.

Ummi's problem page

I think the best way to help friends is to give them the benefit of my many years experience in human relationships. But some people go to great lengths to hide their pain.

Here's a cry for help I found scrawled in a diary under Sanjeev's mattress. I penned a reply right there and then.

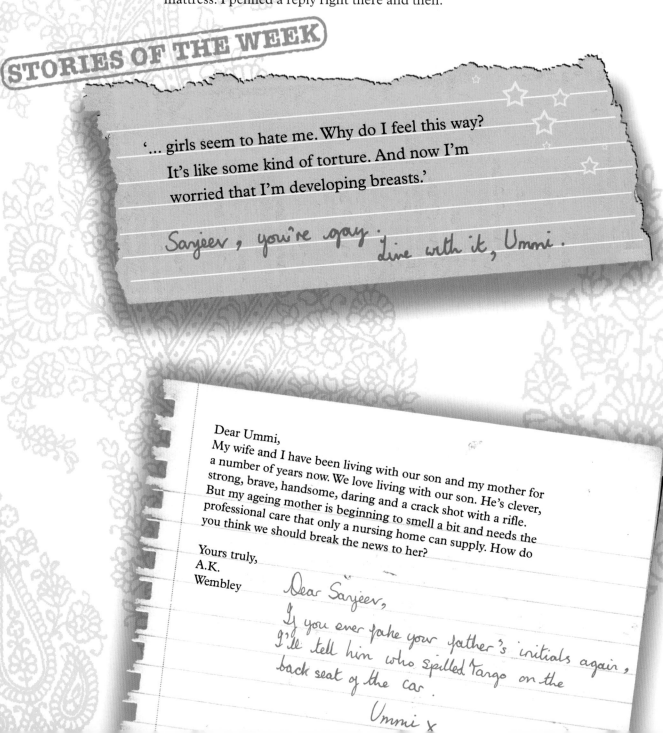

STORIES OF THE WEEK

'... girls seem to hate me. Why do I feel this way? It's like some kind of torture. And now I'm worried that I'm developing breasts.'

Sanjeev, you're gay. Live with it, Ummi.

Dear Ummi,
My wife and I have been living with our son and my mother for a number of years now. We love living with our son. He's clever, strong, brave, handsome, daring and a crack shot with a rifle. But my ageing mother is beginning to smell a bit and needs the professional care that only a nursing home can supply. How do you think we should break the news to her?

Yours truly,
A.K.
Wembley

Dear Sanjeev,
If you ever fake your father's initials again, I'll tell him who spilled Tango on the back seat of the car.

Ummi x

Dear Sushila,

From the moment I met you I've done nothing but think of you. You are the spark in my life, the very essence of love itself. I dream of the day I can bury myself in your passionate embrace. I know there's a big age difference between us, but such things aren't insurmountable. What I lack in years, I can make up for in enthusiasm, energy and sheer acrobatic ability.

Yours for ever, D.H.

For a long time I prayed that this letter was from David Hasselhoff. Well, when we met he couldn't take his eyes off my breasts. Though he could just as easily have been looking at my knees. But every time I go to the grocer's Devinder Heera, the strange young man behind the counter, breaks into a sweat and offers me free *mooli* – so I might be barking up the wrong tree. I wonder what David Hasselhoff did with my reply?

Planning a route

Ashwin Kumar

No one can do more for his fellow man than plan their route. But this is no easy undertaking, so do not shoulder a responsibility like this lightly. Not every Tom, Dick and Harry has the necessary skills to find the best way to get from Bedford to Carlisle without getting snarled up in the M42 gyratory system. It takes a special kind of brain to compute all the variables involved in even the simplest journey. Clearly someone with 'left-brain' logical problem-solving ability. This is no job for someone who's 'creative' or 'empathetic'. And have a think about human physiology. The ideal route planner needs to have a clear view of the map, so the possession of long hair or breasts, for instance, would be a hindrance. They'd always be getting in the way as you picked out A roads etc. So the sort of person who can successfully plan a route should be a) logical and b) not have breasts. I make these guidelines for purely practical reasons, and have no wish to exclude any single group of people. But I think it's obvious that the sort of person who doesn't fulfil these criteria is more of a hindrance than a help.

Before the business of route-planning can begin one must choose a map. Always choose a map that you feel comfortable with, but in my opinion the AA Road Atlas is the prince of cartography. Leather bound, updated yearly and with a small section on Britain's nicest towns it really has got it all. But if you prefer one of the cheaper ring bound versions, help yourself. If you don't mind a map which has a gap between the pages, confusing you at every turn, I'm not going to stand in your way. You just flounder your way across Britain.

A short word needs to be said about Satnav. You are probably thinking 'Ashwin, what's all this fuss about planning a route when these days you can just punch it all into the Satnav and be told where to go?' Well let me ask you a question in turn, smart guy, are you going to let a machine tell you when to go to the bathroom as well? Where is it going to end? It may seem tempting to allow a disembodied female voice to tell you what to do in beautiful clear diction, but it's a temptation that must be avoided at all costs.

So let's say you've had a good look at the map, lingered over the wide open spaces of the AA Road Atlas, traced the blue arteries of our motorways with your index finger, almost feeling the pulse of traffic thrumming along them. Maybe you've allowed your digit to pause on some interesting looking B roads and minor junctions before dismissing them as just a little too poetic. All this before your final decision is made. You've been so thorough and left nothing to chance. So what now can affect your decision-making process? Roadworks!

Roadworks are the snake lurking in the tall grass of efficient journey planning and realisation. The maintenance of our road networks is, of course, a vital function. But there seems to be far too much of it going on and it can blow your journey times clear out of the water. I have a little help here, with my national network of friends to help me. Whenever I'm planning a journey I pick up the phone and give them a bell. So many people have visited our house over the years and accepted our hospitality that I feel I can call them up and ask them about local traffic conditions. Patrick Stewart in particular has been a great help to me – as he tours the country on a combination of stage appearances and Star Trek conventions. I once called him just before he was due onstage at a performance of *Macbeth* and he was able to warn me about a snarl-up just outside Sheffield. He even did it in iambic pentameter – the man's a genius.

Patrick Stewart saved me from a snarl-up outside Sheffield.

Westlife – between them they keep track of roadworks from South Wales to Kent.

Charles Dance knows where to get cheap petrol on the M6.

Who's in charge?

With the route planned and roadworks confirmed you're ready to set off. But the battle is not yet won. If the wrong leader is chosen from a carload of people, only confusion can reign. So who should be the one to be in charge? Who should be the 'Route Captain'? A little bit of self-assessment is needed here and the following little test will help you gauge whether you should be a route planner.

Are you the Route Captain?

Who's in charge? 3 questions

1. **Am I the oldest male person in the car?** (yes/no)

2. **Am I the most practically minded person?** (yes/no)

3. **Do I have the biggest collection of light rock driving music of anyone in the car?** (yes/no)

How did you score?

All yeses You are the Route Captain supreme. All around you should defer to your great knowledge and pathfinding skills. Buy yourself a special Captain's hat and keep it with you at all times.

Two yeses There's potential here. Maybe you can sit up front and hold the map for the Route Captain, or point out speed cameras for them. But don't get over excited and start fiddling with the radio. Leave all controls to the Route Captain. He has full control of the vessel.

All nos Oh dear. You really don't have a clue, and the likelihood is that you are a female passenger. I mean no offence, but the best thing you can do is try to stay out of the way and not demand too many toilet stops. Never, I repeat, never be tempted to offer directions. Even if you are right, it will only cause confusion.

So a properly organised car should have the following layout:

Ballast

Plain sailing

The Route Captain has full control over the driving controls, the route taken, electric windows, and what type of music is played.

The assistant is allowed to sit in the front and hold the map open for the Route Captain, but he must behave.

Avast!

Mutiny!

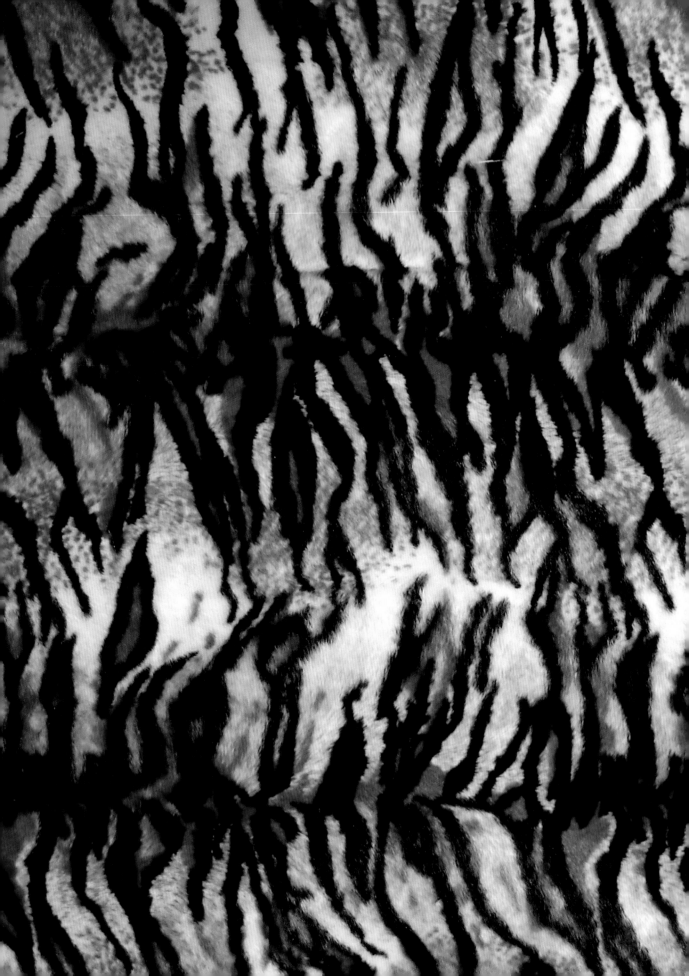

Chapter five
Friends of the
opposite sex:
how does it all work?

The art of seduction

Sanjeev Kumar

Red roses are irresistible – but never eat too many before seducing a lady.

Welcome to the love masterclass. When the makers of this book thought 'Who's going to write the bit about getting it on with the ladies?' I was the natural choice. Though they did ask Dad. And Ummi. And Mum. But I have a feeling that we all know deep down that I am the ultimate ladies' man. I have the eyes, face, neck and upper body of a great lover. I am let down by my legs a bit, which have recently become swollen due to an allergy issue, but the doctors are working on it so no one need worry. Any ladies reading need not fear; I am ready for action anytime, anyplace, anywhere, as long as I have my medication with me. But my love C.V. is littered with famous names – Davina McCall, Minnie Driver, Jodie Kidd, Jane Seymour are all ladies that I have met and even touched. But I thought it would be great to ask my last long-term girlfriend's opinions on how it had been for her. Sort of get the women's perspective on life with 'The Lone Punjabi Wolf'. But I lost touch with Sarah Wilkinson after primary school. I think she's driving a bus these days.

Sanj's top 10 chat-up lines

Let's start with the basics of getting friendly with women. A lot of women tell me they're fed-up of the same cheesy old chat-up lines. That's why I've freshened up some classics and given them the old Sanjy sexing up treatment. It's important to size up your potential new girlfriend and tailor your chat-up line accordingly (although Star Trek remarks work on any girl).

1. Get her phone number
A lot of the time girls get muddled up and give you the wrong number. When this happens and you see them in the same night spot, always go back and ask again. Don't be surprised if this second number is wrong too, they really aren't good with maths. So be patient and keep asking.

2. What star sign are you?
This is a great question because no woman can resist astrology. The trouble comes when they reply and say 'Virgo' or something like that. I have no idea what to say next. Maybe some background research on what each of the star signs means is a good idea.

3. Romantic gestures
Always a hit: one of my best opening lines is to go up to a girl and sing a song. Choose something that you can sing with real feeling. I always do the theme tune to *Star Wars* which goes on for quite a while but is packed with emotion. As an encore I do a Wookie impersonation.

4. Shakespeare
Is there anyone better to quote than the master of love himself, Sir Willhurst Shakespeare? One I like is: 'If music be the food of love, play, play on', because it involves my favourite things: music, food and playing. But if you can't remember long lines there are short quotes like in Act Four, Scene Three of *Hamlet*. The King – who's called Hamlet – says 'Good'. That's a quote anyone can remember. But deliver it very loudly like a king.

5. Women love strong men
Pick up something heavy in their presence. Get some help if you need it; no one needs a bad back, it's murder. When we're on the pull, Sunil and I get each end of a table and move it a bit – it's dynamite.

6. Invitation home

Come back to my place, my parents have probably gone to bed. This speaks for itself, who can resist? Quite a lot of people as it happens.

7. Marvel comics

You'd look a nerd blundering in and asking a girl who her favourite superhero is. So instead, ask her who her favourite 'female' superhero is. It shows you're interested in the same things she's interested in.

8. Fast foods

Casually remark that McDonald's now offer a range of salads so she needn't get any fatter than she already is. This helpful and welcome comment will get you off on the right foot!

9. Dog poo

There seems to be a lot of it about just lately. This could be something you could mention.

10. Nosebleeds

If, like me, you are prone to sudden nosebleeds when stressed, get it out in the open. In fact, why not make it the first thing you say? If you have a bloodstained hanky to show her, all the better.

Now, the biggest rule about seduction is that when you do it properly it doesn't look like seduction at all. For instance, I can meet a girl, have a drink with her, go for a nice meal and it would come as a total surprise to her that we were 'going out' or 'an item'. That's just one example of why I am known as Smooth Sanjy up and down the kebab houses of old Wembley High Street. I'll tell you a bit more about that later on – when I show you how to get and keep a girlfriend for up to twelve hours. But for now, settle in and relax as I guide you through the gentle art of making it with a hottie.

Meeting women

I live by the motto 'wham bam thank you ma'am' … yes, a minor motor collision is an excellent way to meet women. Unfortunately, Dad won't let me drive his car because I'm still on a provisional licence so I take my BMX down to the traffic lights on the North Circular. As soon as I see a hot lady stop at a red light, I slip the bike into gear, pedal as quick as I can into her front wing and sprawl myself onto the bonnet. They nearly always get out of the car to check I'm OK. If you're really lucky she might touch your knee and ask you if you're alright. Result.

Body language

If you're past stage one, and actually meeting women naturally in public places without using a bike collision as an ice-breaker, then you know how important body language is. Body language is communication without the need for words – like winking or making kissy noises with your lips. When you first see a lady across a room, keep an open body posture, arms wide open, feet apart. This makes you seem welcoming and open to approach. The overall effect can be enhanced by offering her a bite of your kebab.

Humour

You know you're getting somewhere when you make a woman laugh. Though subtle humour is not such a good idea in a nightclub situation. Many is the time I've dropped in one of my Wildesque quips while I'm sitting with a lady only for them to burst out laughing minutes later when I'm cutting it on the dance floor. They've only just got it, you see. So if you're in a nightclub or loud bar, stick to visual comedy. Me and Sunil have a whole slapstick routine worked out for when we're on the pull. Sunil holds a plank and pretends he can't see me, then as he turns round I have to keep ducking. It is hilarious. Now, we've just got to come up with a way of getting the plank into a nightclub.

Eye contact

The eyes are the window of your soul, and are your best way of
conveying how you feel. I mentioned winking earlier – which is a great
way of subtly giving the right signals to a girl. But you should develop
some more 'looks'. I mean, just staring at a girl won't get you anywhere
on its own. Staring is just the beginning, after that you have to raise the
game. For instance a lot of women say I have 'come to bed' eyes.

Come to bed eyes.

Unwanted advances

Sooner or later we guys have to deal with unwelcome attention. It's a shame, but there are times when ladies come on a little too strong and put a man off. I'm no stranger to this – I've got a couple of Aunties who always try to kiss me disconcertingly on the lips whenever they come round. It's horrible and one of them has a mole. My advice is to hide in your room until they've gone.

Chocolates

It's a scientific fact that women like chocolates so this is definitely a romantic gift. But use it with caution. If you're going out with a larger girl, choose low-cal alternatives like yoghurt raisins and tell her why. This way she knows you're sensitive to her weight issues and a modern man.

Commitment

Women are always looking for the big C, isn't it? Whereas blokes like to play around the field or, in my case, the park. How do you balance these up when you're seducing a woman? My approach is honesty. If you meet a woman, tell her you're looking for a short-term no-strings thing before she gets any ideas. Does it work? Well, I've never been saddled with a long-term girlfriend, so work it out for yourself.

Kumars Sutra

Ummi

Hello darlings, and welcome to my guide to getting horizontal. Actually I mean that literally. I have tremendous trouble trying to get into bed and unlocking my hips so I can straighten my back. What girl hasn't been through the trauma of things hotting up in the bedroom only to be let down by 'frozen vertebrae'?

But help is at hand. Here's my sure-fire way of getting yourself straightened out and ready for action.

1) Ok, so I'm sitting on the bed.

2) You see the problem now?

3) I just need a little help.

4) Ouch! Now I'm ready for action.

If this has been of some help, write in for my factsheet on how to overcome that other 'passion killer' – abdominal gas.

How to get a girlfriend and keep her for up to 12 hours

Sanjeev Kumar

Would it surprise you to learn that none of my relationships last very long? I often ask myself why this is. But the answer's staring me right in the mirror. No woman can handle the Lone Punjabi Wolf for any length of time. Ummi says no woman has ever handled the Lone Punjabi Wolf full stop, and she could be right. See, when I've had my fill, I toss them aside like one of those plastic burger boxes. Though I'm careful to scrape out any remaining shredded lettuce and ketchup. No sense in waste, isn't it? The box that is, I don't like women covered in shredded lettuce and ketchup. Though I do quite fancy the girl who works at Burger King – but I worry it's not because of who she is, but what she does. Which is no basis for a stable relationship. Ummi says one of the reasons women can't cope with me is that 'there's too much "man" packed into this compact frame – two stones too much' and for once I'm inclined to agree with her. When I weigh in on the scales of love, I'm in the super-heavyweight class.

So how does The Sanjmeister handle a typical relationship? Well Ummi's bet me a fiver I can't find and hang on to a girlfriend for twelve hours. No problemo. Here's twelve hours in a typical relationship for me.

12:00pm midday

I start my cruising in KFC at the shopping precinct, with Ummi. You can watch the shoppers go by, you can eat chicken and you're sitting with your grandmother so you don't look like some lonely loser.

12:30pm

Hello, hello! A group of young ladies has taken a table nearby. I pick one out and give her 'the eye'. She looks over at me and gives me 'the finger'. Eye contact – result!

12:37pm

It's hotting up. All the girls at the table have gone, leaving the last one on her own. It's time to move. Action stations. All engines on and maximum thrust. Sanjeev Airlines flight number 007 to Ladyland is cleared for take off.

12:48pm

I can't think what I'll say. Oh I know.

12:51pm

I walk past her table and pretend to drop my wallet. When I bend over she gets a great view of my bum. I hold the position for just long enough to arouse her interest. Then I let her know casually that the old woman I'm sitting with is my grandmother, not my date.

12:51:30seconds

She makes a run for it. This happens a lot when women are confronted suddenly with my raw sex appeal. They run like frightened animals. This one drops her purse so she'll come back for it. No, she just keeps going. I guess she knows I'll return it to her later – which means that we're going out! Lucky for her, it's got her mobile number in it.

1:00pm

Lunchtime. Chicken Wings – after which go home and have short nap.

6:00pm

Wake up after short nap. Remember I'm in a relationship which means I have to report in to 'the boss' or 'she who must be obeyed'. Girls, eh?

6:05pm

Give her a ring on the mobile. She screams abuse at me and tells me to **** off. Phew, it must be her 'time' or something. I give her some space.

6:10pm

I give her another bell to check she's OK. She hangs up. Well, if that's the way she wants it – this one is going to have to learn the hard way. She wants to play that game, let's see who cracks first.

6:15pm

She's switched her mobile off.

6:17pm

I try calling her, but accidentally dial a pizza delivery number instead. I order a pizza.

6:45pm

Pizza arrives.

6:46pm

Eaten it.

7:00pm

I'm getting tired of these 'mind games'. If she can't respect me then maybe it's time we called it a day. I leave her a message telling her it's over and I only ever went out with her for a bet, anyway.

7:05pm

I leave her a message saying I've forgiven her and we should give it another go.

8:00pm

Well she hasn't called back so it must be on again. It's great having a steady girlfriend. I wonder what she's doing now.

10:00 am the next day

I wake to the smell of bacon and a lady asking me how I like my eggs. Sunny side up, Mum! Check the mobile – no messages from my girlfriend. Looks like Ummi owes me a fiver,

Ummi's romantic tips

Ummi

Things have changed a lot in the world of romance since I was a young girl courting in my village in India. Smooching, public fondling and dirty phone chat are things that as a girl were either unheard of or forbidden.

Fortunately, these days I can make up for those lost years by indulging as much as I like. But in an Indian village, there were very few opportunities for a growing girl to learn about love and tenderness and even less about the trouser area of men. In fact, in village life men were in short supply. I spent my youth practising chat-up lines on livestock, who never understood a word of what I was saying. Though I did get to first base with a goat once ... but that's another story.

The question you ask yourself is how did I go from being a goat-struck village girl to the slick operator and man magnet that I am now? The answer resides with my teenage friend Srsvathi the Bicycle. Srsvathi was always curious about the world and one day she had been rummaging around in her father's almari where she found an illustrated text on the noble art of the courtesan. We used to meet by twilight under the branches of the banyan tree and pore over its pages. There we learned that in ancient Indian culture, the courtesan was a figure of great respect and dignity. They were women who were well versed in poetry, the fine arts and giving love bites. It was an episode that changed our lives. Particularly Srsvathi's because it was from this point she earned the 'bicycle' part of her moniker. And I can tell you it has nothing to do with the Tour de France, though she did once tour France with a troupe of acrobats ... but that's another story. I took things at a slightly slower pace than my friend. But my new-found skills were to be seen all over the village, until my father told me to stop biting the livestock.

Well, after that I had the confidence to talk to boys and make boyfriends. My first such boyfriend was a wild and romantic figure who travelled from town to town, village to village as free as a bird. It was the local milk-man, or *Doodh-wallah*. He cut a dashing sight with his churns strapped to the sides of his bicycle, pedalling furiously to get over the hill. I used to meet him after his round and he'd take me to the cinema, which was very exciting. In the close company of the dark theatre the magic of the screen would fill our minds with romantic images of kings and queens, robbers and policemen, dancing girls and princes. And I began to ask myself what I was doing with a man whose idea of a romantic gift was a bottle of warm milk and who smelt of paneer cheese? Everything I had dreamed of was flickering across a canvas screen beckoning me into the world of entertainment. So I threw him over and asked out the projectionist instead. Free film tickets, you can't beat it.

All this hanky panky came to a stop when I got married. A long chapter in my life. But not worth going into in detail as it was mainly boring.

These days, I'm back on form and have had a number of on-screen dalliances with big-name celebrities. Who can forget the time I had Robson Green in my bedroom? The poor mite looked terrified but he shouldn't have worried, I was going to be gentle with him. Sadly for both of us we were interrupted by Ashwin before I managed to work my charm.

The one that got away.

Martin Kemp was another cheeky dish I had my eye on. The former singer and soap star was giving me all the right signals and I thought I was definitely 'in there'. I started with some saucy comments and a bit of groping – you know the subtle stuff – before inviting him up to my room after the show. He promised me he would come, but I waited in vain for a couple of hours before my body stocking began to itch, and I had to abandon it. He doesn't know what he missed.

Another one that got away.

When Westlife came on the show I thought all my prayers had been answered all at once with interest and a double dollop of cream.
I remember saying to myself 'If I can't persuade one of these innocent young men into my room I'm not the woman I think I am.' I turned out not to be the woman I think I am. I had said it out loud and Ashwin heard me. After that he kept a very careful eye on them. It was torture, like a wolf watching hungrily at a parade of fresh lamb hoping for a straggler.

A whole bunch that also got away.

Well those are the stories of just a few of my conquests. Maybe you are an older woman tempted to use some of my techniques to further your own love life. I wish you every success, just don't do it anywhere near Wembley. I don't need the competition.

How to keep a relationship alive

Ashwin Kumar

After so many years of happy marriage, people often ask me what the secret is. The answer is simple, we had an arranged marriage and we come from a generation that feels it's wrong to divorce even if our lives are a living hell. I'm just kidding. Madhuri and I have sufficient amounts of liking for one another and we are perfectly happy. But how is this stability achieved? Not without significant expense and effort on my part, let me tell you. The following is my advice on how to keep the flame of your marriage burning as brightly as ours.

Share your interests

No marriage gets far before the question of interests arises. Men and women may have very different outlooks on life but I'm fortunate that Madhuri and I share similar tastes. For instance, on the occasion of our fifteenth wedding anniversary I took Madhuri to Photocopier 2000. The look on her face when I told her where we were going!

Madhuri's face when I told her about Photocopier 2000.

And when I took her to Biro-Fest at the NEC for our 26th anniversary.

And when I took her to World of Calculators for our 27th anniversary.

A trip to the cinema

What could be more romantic than a trip to the cinema? The whole experience evokes the pleasures of youth and is guaranteed to refresh your relationship. Of course the choice of film is very important. No man wants to sit through two hours of drivel starring Julia Roberts trying to marry someone who she's not suited to. So I took Madhuri to see *Downfall* – which is about the last days of Hitler in his bunker. She was utterly speechless so I knew I had hit the right tone. Fascinating film. Did you know that not only did Hitler kill himself but also gave a suicide pill to his favourite Alsatian, Blondie? I wish I could do that to Mr Aggarwal's Alsatian, but he'd probably have a chunk out of my arm!

After I took her to see 'Downfall'.
I think I won some Brownie points there.

Take her to a restaurant

Nothing gives you a better chance to really spend time talking with one another than going out for a meal. Which is why I avoid restaurants like the plague. But if you are cornered, try not to see it as a sacrifice. Instead, make a game out of it. See how little you can persuade your partner to eat. A side salad is a perfectly good main dish while a well-timed comment about her weight will save you the cost of dessert. And always quibble about the bill. Even if it is correct they'll often knock a bit off just to stop you embarrassing them.

Create a romantic mood

Every so often I like to do something special for Madhuri at home.
I prepare her a romantic meal to eat by candle-light. In the flickering
flame, our stomachs sated on Tesco's tagliatelle, I wonder how much
longer such a perfect moment can last. I wish it would go on for eternity
– you see I've figured out that I'm saving myself a fortune by having all
the lights out. Work it out yourselves – ten lightbulbs, 80 watts each for
an entire evening. We must be looking at two or three kilowatt hours!
I don't think I've ever felt so aroused.

Mini break

The mini break is the prince of all romantic gestures. Two nights in
one of Europe's capitals. I always book a three-star hotel with breakfast
included. Eat enough from the buffet and who needs lunch or dinner?
Rome, Berlin, Barcelona, we've done them all. But I draw the line
at Paris, it's too close to Brussels. The thought of those bureaucrats
dreaming up more red tape with which to strangle the small
businessman. It would make the complementary cereals turn
to ash in my mouth.

Have some 'me' time

Having time to yourself is important in any relationship. Often when
Madhuri is talking I completely shut down, allowing me to recharge my
batteries while Madhuri gets some old nonsense or other 'off her chest'.

That's really all there is to it. Striking a balance between displays of
affection and watching TV, with the occasional restaurant meal thrown
in. I wish you a happy and long marriage.

I shut down completely and recharge my batteries.

How useful has this book been to you?

Well, you've read the book, but how far have you come on the road to being more like the Kumars? Take a little time to answer this self-assessment questionnaire to find out how much more emotionally and mentally stable you are and which of the Kumars you have become most like.

How do you feel after reading this book?

 Hungry   Wealthy

 Nice   Old

In which area do you think you most improved because of this book?

 My ability to eat more

 My accountancy and DIY skills

 My tidying up

 My knitting

How would you recommend this book to a friend?

 Delicious

 Inexpensive

 Clean

 Large lettering

Where do you see your life leading now you've read this book?

 To the fridge

 To my warehouse

 To my kitchen

 To the toilet

How would you like you see yourself in five years' time?

 Fighting aliens on a space station with Sunil

 Running a multinational commercial empire

 Running a clean house – but slightly bigger than the Aggarwals'

 Still being alive

Which situations would you handle differently having read this book?

 I have the confidence to tackle a large burglar. Or a large burger

 I have the confidence to pull off a financial scam

 I have the confidence to 'shake 'n vac'

 I have the confidence to grope David Hasselhoff

Well, that little test should tell you a lot about yourself and which of the Kumars you have become most like. Happy eating/shelving/cleaning/steradenting!

Love
The Kumars

If you have enjoyed this book, you may also wish to read:
The River Less Paddled   *I'm Okay –You, I Don't Know*
Beach Trips in a Landlocked Country   *Da Rolf Harris Code*